Kate and H

THE MYSTIC GARDEN

'A pathway to another world' (p. 121): Sheffield Park.

The Mystic Garden

Douglas Swinscow

Illustrations by Cynthia Rowan

First published in Great Britain in 1992 by The Halsgrove Press

Copyright © Douglas Swinscow, 1992

All rights reserved. No part of this publication may be reproduced, stored in a retrieval system, or transmitted in any form or by any means, without the prior permission of the copyright holder.

British Library Cataloguing in Publication Data
CIP Catalogue Record for this book is available from the British Library

ISBN 1 874448 00 0

The Halsgrove Press
Chinon Court
Lower Moor Way
Tiverton EX16 6SS
Tel: 0884 243242
Fax: 0884 243325

Designed for The Halsgrove Press by
Topic Visual Information,
397 Topsham Road, EXETER EX2 6HD (0392) 876800

Typeset by
Exe Valley, Exeter, Devon

Printed and bound in Great Britain by
BPCC Wheatons Ltd, Exeter, Devon

To Josephine,

for over 50 years my loving wife and witty companion

By the same author:

Statistics at Square One
Macrolichens of East Africa (with Professor H. Krog)
Reap a Destiny (autobiography)

Contents

List of Illustrations

Preface

SOME of the old Buddhist temples in Japan have a veranda from which visitors may view the garden. It may be a simple platform, but often it is a complex of several platforms threading their way through the garden and allowing visitors to examine the scene from different viewpoints. While standing (without shoes) to contemplate a temple garden I have noticed Buddhist visitors beside me kneeling in prayer.

This sacred communion with the world of nature, God's handiwork, has faded from most peoples' lives in Britain today. Yet it was not always so.

In the Georgian era of the eighteenth and early nineteenth centuries the great gardens and parks may not have inspired their visitors to kneel and pray, because the Christian religion sets a different context for our prayer. But those great artificial landscapes did offer a philosophical vision that still has power to move us. Even today they give us a glimpse of eternal human values as they are symbolised for us in nature. Nature itself has no values, but in a garden it can present a symbolic world that deepens our understanding of the real world.

This was brought home to me when I was visiting Stourhead in Wiltshire. A woman walking ahead of me turned to a friend at her side and said, 'I often come here – it's so *peaceful.*' A small thing and probably a common experience. Yet in a few words she reached to something that lay far deeper than the world of garden centres, 'plantsman's gardens', or displays of scarce species (sometimes taken illicitly from the wild). These are the bane of twentieth century gardening in Britain, where horticulture as an end in itself and the emphasis in many catalogues on the rarity of species and varieties to tempt the purchaser's pride, have swamped what used to be the true role of a garden, namely, to give expression to its owner's soul. That is the theme of this book.

As a scientist I know that the study of the universe by the scientific method is the best way we have of obtaining valid answers to some of the questions we ask about it. But there are other questions, commonly asked and of deep significance to each of us and to mankind as a whole, that are outside the range of scientific inquiry. Some of them are touched on in this book.

A veneration for the natural underpins all the comments I make here on gardens. I believe that an understanding of nature beyond the purely scientific or rational, together with respect for its ways, can help to make clearer the context of our existence in the universe. When we ponder on the 'meaning of life' we use a phrase that has no meaning for professional philosophers. But for the ordinary person it subsumes a great deal of his perplexity in the face of the unknown and of his doubt about his own destiny. Contemplating some gardens with the eye of faith, we may attain to a liberation of the self into something much greater, such as many religious mystics have described, an attunement with the music of the spheres and fulfilment at our journey's end.

But the mystic garden is not a substitute for religion: it is complementary to it. The love of nature and the worship of God go hand in hand.

'A sense of communion with nature' (p. 10): Savill garden.

CHAPTER ONE

The Spire

AS a father and grandfather I know that gardens serve many purposes. Children play in them, the dog has his runs, the cat digs holes, the potatoes are grown, the washing hangs out, and the rabbit lurks in his hutch. But in some gardens the needs of the household are less urgent. One gardener may use his* land to carry out genetic experiments, or, at a simpler intellectual level, applies his technical skill to breed plants which he hopes will win him prizes at the horticultural show. Another gardener may so design his garden as to make of it a work of art. His object is to provide pleasure to the senses, whether from the visual display of colour and form, the mingling of scents, the play of light and shade, or the glitter of a fountain. And to a third gardener it is a

* The English language long ago set an example to its European neighbours in getting rid of gender from almost all words, but of those few which still do have a gender much the most troublesome are the personal pronouns and adjectives, he/she, his/hers. Rather than pepper the text with these verbal hiccups, as has become the fashion in some quarters I simply use the male form in the knowledge that I am dealing with grammatical gender, not biological sex (the absurdity of speaking of *people* as having a gender has unfortunately now invaded our language). Likewise 'man' and 'mankind' have their time-honoured meaning of including women as well as men.

symbolic vision of another world that he tries to achieve – a vision that perhaps conjures up associations with the perfection and innocence of the Garden of Eden, or with the assurance of the Augustan age of Rome; or he may have put his imagination to the expression of his own personal vision of life.

These three approaches to the garden are respectively the intellectual, the aesthetic, and the religious. In the intellectual category the emphasis is on horticulture undertaken for technical ends (breeding winners, for example) or for the purposes of scientific inquiry or simply for enjoyment. The aesthetic category of gardening ranges from the deliberate creation of works of art to nothing more abstruse than sensory delight in colourful flowerbeds or a handful of plums on a warm afternoon. It is the religious category that is most likely to puzzle today's readers. Here I am not speaking exclusively about any of the organised religions, whether Christianity or Buddhism or Judaism or Islam (among many others), but of a faculty which I believe most people have for recognising a sacred element in the universe and responding to it through channels which may be those ordinarily regarded as religious, or in ways outside the conventional channels altogether.

We may, I believe, draw spiritual inspiration from our world, just as we may enjoy aesthetic pleasure in it or treat it as an object of intellectual study. Some things are sacred, others beautiful, and yet others rational. No doubt the sensitivity to these qualities varies from one person to another, and it can certainly be enhanced by education and practice. What is important is the absolute distinction between the three ways: intellectual, aesthetic, spiritual.

The essence of the scientific method is that, by observation and experiment, it produces results whose validity can be tested. They can be confirmed or refuted or held to need further testing. Sometimes they can be expressed only as a probability, which can be specified. Experience has shown that conclusions reached by the scientific method are only an approximation to a more general understanding of the truth. Further work with new ideas or different material or more delicate instruments will lead to a closer approximation, a more comprehensive understanding of the subject.

Thus three categories; and to confuse the methods and aims of one with those of another is disastrous. Yet the same mental faculties in varying proportions go into all of them: sensory perception, reasoning, feeling, intuition, will power, belief, imagination. Research scientists use their imagination just as much as artists do and act on belief just like religious people. So too the artists and religious people are guided by reason and the will to reach a goal in the same way as scientists. It is the methods they use and the end products that differ.

Yet occasionally there is a true rapprochement between art and science that does not degenerate into a debased medley of both. As an example a fine suspension bridge such as the one spanning the Avon gorge may be cited. It is both beautiful and perfectly engineered; but, more than that, the beauty and the engineering are indissolubly an expression of the fulfilment of the needs that the bridge meets. Here Keats would have recognised that 'Beauty is truth, truth beauty.'

★ ★ ★

The impetus given to art by Christianity, and to Christianity by art, throughout the centuries bears witness to the value of this particular conjunction. Time and again each has been inspired and refreshed by the other. But on occasions when their roles were confused and art became a substitute for religion, or religion for art, the consequence was the debasement of each.

As an example of a human creation that may be looked at in this tripartite manner we can consider the spire of Salisbury Cathedral. It is possible to describe it entirely in mathematical and engineering terms, and doubtless its architects in the fourteenth century did so specify it when they planned and oversaw its construction. Yet aesthetically it must be judged one of the supreme triumphs of Gothic art, in its slender proportions taking architecture to such limits of aspiration as can be expressed in masonry. And more than all that, it has a spiritual aura partly because it crowns a great church and partly in so far as its form gives symbolic expression so forcefully to man's yearning to reach up to the heavens. Indeed as the Dean and Chapter have recorded,[1] 'these buildings are not only *places* of worship, they are in themselves *acts* of worship'.

Though a scientist, I see what may be described as the work of God throughout creation. This does not mean that I am arguing in defence of pantheism, namely that everything in the universe is actually a part of God and so deserves the kind of worship that religions prescribe for God himself (or herself; God has no sexual orientation, yet can hardly be described as 'it'). We may deeply respect all living creatures, and all inanimate nature too such as rocks and rivers and glittering ores, but that is not to be confused with the worship that man devotes to God.

Nor, in speaking of the works of God, am I implying that anything in the universe is beyond scientific scrutiny and interpretation. But if the whole universe, or even a microcosm of it represented by a garden, can be interpreted in scientific terms of cause and effect and inference, why bring in God? In rational argument I would answer this question by reference to what we know so far about the origin of the universe and time. Cosmologists tell us it began with a sudden explosion that created space and time and their material contents. To ask what existed before the 'big bang' is a meaningless question to science. Yet I believe it not meaningless to suppose that the big bang happened in something, an antecedent state or condition or force, something we may think of as God, while at the same time we acknowledge that this thought springs from an act of faith, not of reason.

'There was something formless yet incomplete
That existed before heaven and earth;
Without sound, without substance,
Dependent on nothing, unchanging,
All pervading, unfailing.
One may think of it as the mother of all things under heaven.'

Tao Tê Ching, ch. 25.[2]

Why make this act of faith? Man's reason sees the cathedral spire in one context as an engineering achievement; his aesthetic faculty thrills to its beauty; his spirit soars with it towards the heavens, freed from the prison of his earthbound self. Three distinct approaches to it: and with something like the skill of an orchestral conductor we may, without confusing them, achieve a unison of understanding such that each enriches the other. And so with a garden: we may analyse its soil, classify the design architecturally, define the plants botanically, grade the colours of its flowers by colour charts, and present the results in a historical perspective – all necessary enough studies. But can the garden give us anything more? Can it draw from us a sense of communion with nature or impart to us a deeper understanding of ourselves? Since I look upon nature as ultimately the creation of God, my exploration of a garden is a quest for his spirit.

CHAPTER TWO

A Symbolic Journey

AS an example of a garden with several mystic features we may consider Castle Drogo in Devon. It was completed in 1929 in accordance with a design by Sir Edwin Lutyens, architect of the castle. For the original planting scheme Gertrude Jekyll was consulted, but the proposals submitted by George Dillistone, of Tunbridge Wells, were preferred. The National Trust now owns it and keeps it in beautiful condition.

Lying quite separately from the castle and invisible from it, the garden is laid out on ground sloping to the south. But unfortunately, owing to the necessity of guiding in a smooth flow the many people who visit the garden, the majority are tempted to enter it from the wrong end. Consequently, though they enjoy the azaleas in the spring and the roses in summer, they see it all backwards and cannot have any idea of the mystic experience it offers.

The correct way to enter the Drogo garden is from the lower, southern end, near the castle. We walk into a dark tunnel of beech trees and, still within the tunnel, ascend a flight of steps. In the semi-darkness our everyday world is blacked out, our thoughts are stilled, our expectancy is heightened. As we mount the quite steep steps through the trees, we feel that the effort required makes us more alert and sharpens our readiness to experience the new world at the top.

We go through a gate, step forward a couple of paces, and there suddenly the garden is displayed all around, a *coup de théâtre*. Virtually the whole garden lies before us. With a strong resemblance to the excavated foundations of a Roman palace, the garden has a strictly rectangular plan, with walls to the left and right and ahead, and a further flight of steps in the centre of the opposite wall leading to a path sloping upwards on the axis through our viewpoint.

As we stand at the end of the tunnel and examine the view before us we see a parterre bounded by the walls and patterned with squares of rose beds and beautifully kept grass. At the four corners of the parterre are little rooms of clipped yew roofed with trained *Parrotia persica*. Above the level of the walls at either side and at the far end, forming a second storey at walltop level, are beds of herbaceous plants. Incidentally the pattern with which they are edged was suggested to Lutyens by Indian architecture. You may stroll through the rose garden to the steps at the far end, or you may reach them by going up on either side above the walls and walking alongside the herbaceous borders. From there too you get an excellent view of the parterre over the tops of the herbaceous plants.

Ascending the flight of steps at the end of the rose garden, you enter a straight path bordered by informal trees and shrubs. These include Japanese maples, magnolias, and azaleas, filling the air with their scents in spring. The final walk up the path again demands a slight exertion that concentrates the imagination in readiness to receive the next impression. At its upper end you go through a gap in a tall yew hedge and see spread before you – what? Nothing but a vast circular lawn bounded by an evergreen hedge of some magnificence.

The sense of enclosure, of shelter, in the garden is heightened by the tall trees that surround it, mostly beeches and oaks. They and the walls bounding the parterre give us the comfort of privacy and of being cut off from the outer world. On this stormy hillside at 850 feet (260m) altitude we have a safe refuge. And this belief is reinforced by the geometrical character of the garden's design. These clearcut lines, bold steps, neat squares of lawn and rose beds, the straight vista through the garden that confronts us as we step into it from the dark tunnel – all combine to present to us an assured place in the natural world. That we can also receive from nature a feeling of assurance by quite different means will become apparent below, but here the symbol of an underlying order in nature is that idealisation of natural forms and relations that we call geometry.

In this garden we see in a fully developed form the theme of rebirth leading to enlightenment. We are initiated into its mystery by ascending the first flight of steps through the tunnel of beeches. Here art and nature combine to draw a curtain over the mind's seething images and preconceptions. The old world is shut out; a new world awaits us. Stepping into the garden at the end of the tunnel we suddenly enter a separate, secluded, embracing, idealised palace of nature, a world of geometry, order, certitude.

Là, tout n'est qu'ordre et beauté,
Luxe, calme et volupté.
C. Baudelaire, *L'invitation au voyage.*

Crossing the parterre we absorb the rectilinear pattern of its rose beds, grass blocks, and boundary walls. Though it is all far from natural, a relationship with nature's apparently casual disposition is maintained by the planting of the walls, whose crevices are filled with a variety of flowering plants and ferns. The geometry of the scene enters the mind and generates a harmonious framework in which our worries and doubts are reduced to order, our enthusiasms given a sharper focus.

After traversing the garden, its parterre, steps, and inclined path, we pass expectantly through the formal hedge and enter – nothing but a circular lawn. Then we understand: *nothing* is the source and the end of *everything*. Each is at the node of an ever changing cycle of life, death, life, death . . .

CHAPTER THREE

The Nature of Nature

ONE of mankind's most enduring myths, found in one form or another among peoples all round the world, is that we are descended from ancestors who in a distant past lived wholly natural lives. They were free of care, filled with innocent joy, spontaneous in their relationships, helpful to each other, peaceful in their ambitions, and in harmony with the animal and vegetable kingdoms. The animals and plants too enjoyed a state of perfect equilibrium. None encroached upon another's territory, and none preyed upon another except for the natural necessity of obtaining food – and then only in a manner acceptable to the tender hearted poets who recorded their vision. The Gardens of the Hesperides, where the golden apples grew, and the Garden of Eden, whose apples were a more troublesome gift to mankind, had their counterpart in almost every culture.

With the growth of a scientific outlook in the western world from the seventeenth century onwards the Garden of Eden began to fade into dreamland. Expeditions no longer set sail to discover it, as they had done till then. While nature would have been a religious conception to a fourteenth century European, filled with emblems of sanctity and wickedness, concupiscence and bawdy jokes, evil spirits and alarming apparitions, by the seventeenth and eighteenth centuries it became a source of aesthetic enjoyment in the paintings of Claude Lorraine, Nicolas Poussin, Watteau, van Ruisdael, Richard Wilson, Aelbert Cuyp, and many lesser artists, while to the great landowners it was a domain to be improved by the latest agricultural techniques then being actively developed.

* * *

Open any book on the history of gardens and you will find Horace Walpole[1] quoted as saying of William Kent: 'He leaped the fence, and saw that all nature was a garden.' Walpole's observations on the design of gardens and parks, their history and their aesthetic qualities, are of lively interest today. He wrote of rivers and bowers, parterres, fountains, the clumping of trees, symmetry and asymmetry, and the smoothness of lawns among many aspects of his subject. But what did he know of nature? Or mean by it? His further remarks[1] on Kent give us a clue:

> *'He felt the delicious contrast of hill and valley changing imperceptibly into each other, tasted the beauty of the gentle swell, or concave scoop, and remarked how loose groves crowned an easy eminence with happy ornament, and while they called in the distant view between their graceful stems, removed and extended their perspective by delusive comparison.'*

Looking out of a library or drawing room window Walpole, wherever he happened to be visiting, was likely to see a regularly cultivated landscape where the contours of hills and valleys were gentle and the meadows colourful with wild flowers, where hedges lay in trim but not too straight lines, and clumps of woodland added their picturesque decoration to the scene. Indeed, as Sir Keith Thomas[2] has put it,

'the scene was only called a "landscape" because it was reminiscent of a painted "landskip"; it was "picturesque" because it looked like a picture.'

As the swamps were drained and the forests cleared what had formerly seemed to be hostile tracts of nature became benign and fertile tracts. The enclosed fields and woods represented nature transformed, though still nature. But by the time Walpole wrote (1771) and published (1780) the words quoted above livelier spirits had moved on to wilder horizons.

The taste for nature as 'landskip' was already giving way to an enthusiasm for 'rude' scenes in North Wales, the English Lakes, and the Scottish Highlands, where travellers even risked their necks among slippery gullies and falling rocks. Visits to the Swiss Alps soon followed to provide a yet rougher contact with nature. At the end of the seventeenth century well cultivated, fertile fields seemed to display nature at her best; by the end of the eighteenth century their role was reversed: they seemed wholly unnatural in contrast to the now admired mountains, gorges, cliffs, and forests.

Today we acknowledge sadly that nature in a pristine state is hard to find. We think of ourselves as standing outside it, even though occasionally we have qualms about whether we shall suffer a cataclysmic fate of the kind we have seen

'A regularly cultivated landscape where the contours of hills and valleys were gentle' (p. 17): Petworth.

overtaking other species so often in the fossil record. Out there is the great assemblage of the Earth's plants and animals, its mountains and rivers, its seas swarming from top to bottom with life, and the fossils in layer upon layer of rocks deposited throughout vast ages. Our self-consciousness sets us apart from the abundance of living species – thrusting, munching reproducing – yet in most of us lurks a desire to feel we have a role in the natural drama. We speak of a sense of kinship with nature and strive to achieve some kind of harmony with it through walking in wild places, or gazing at the sky, or sailing and swimming, or in creating gardens. But if Walpole's nature was a delusion, what is ours?

* * *

Nature is not in harmony with itself. If it were, evolution would have ceased long ago, and the fossil record shows it has never done so. This fragmentary record, though it gives us no more than a glimpse of life in past times, does show one unequivocal feature, and that is unceasing change; change of form, of life strategy, of prevalence, perpetual change and perpetual conflict. Predators and parasites dominate the record, eating their way through species after species till a gap is opened for another species to fill, only for itself to be dislodged by successors and finally obliterated from the earth.

Nor, in many parts of the world, does nature wear an aspect that could offer any kind of inspiration to a garden maker. Sandy and rocky deserts, arid steppes, and mountain corries under ice and snow, though often intensely beautiful and biologically rich, are not the sort of natural habitats from which a gardener can draw ideas, and when he attempts to do so he fails: no scree garden supports the tapestry of life to be seen in a natural scree, no alpine garden the beauty of an evolved community defying the elements in an alpine outcrop of rocks.

Here then is a paradox we seek to resolve. Despite the inferences to be drawn from the fossil record, we see, in the short span of our own lives, nature as an intricate balance of living organisms fitting neatly into the template of their environment, at home in forest and moraine, sand dune and sea cliff, montane meadow and river valley, snow patch and rock cleft, moorland and stony ridge. And we long to feel part of this apparently harmonious family.

Yet we know the harmony to be a dream that harks back through the unceasing conflict of ages to the lost innocence of man's childhood. In reality every daisy on the lawn is struggling for space among the grasses, and every rose bush is mustering its hormones to fight off the mildew attack. The tree at the end of the garden is surrounded by bare patches where it has shaded its herbaceous competitors out of existence. The ferns in the wall have fallen victim to a succession of droughts, and their crevices are taken over by sedum.

This is not the nature we contemplate in the hope of quenching our thirst from its well of tranquillity. So we create a garden that symbolises the abundance of life by the variety of plants that we grow in it, the harmony of life by our setting aside the space that each plant requires for its full development, and the fulfilment of life by encouraging the formation of flowers and setting of fruit; and by making it beautiful we attempt to enhance our communion with nature through the medium of aesthetic pleasure. It is an idea, a dream, a Garden of Eden, where every plant has its appropriate place and role, and where all who visit it can draw spiritual refreshment from feeling themselves to be part of a great natural symphony.*

If in its design the mystic garden represents an ideal rather than the reality of nature, we should take pains to cultivate the plants in it so that they individually may reach towards their ideal form. But what is that ideal form? It is certainly not a form attained by growing the plant in isolation from other plants as though it were being grown for exhibition. All nature lives in communities, and plants interact with each other. Their pressures and demands give character to themselves and their neighbours. When grown in perfect conditions in a greenhouse or under a little umbrella to protect them from rain and sun and frost, they may be better prepared for the show bench. But their features show no emotion, no striving, no gaining, no yielding, no suffering, and no joy of living. They are blank.

* * *

The education that a garden gives a child may be of lifelong value.† Like everything else to which he is exposed it moulds his mind the more indelibly for the tenderness of his senses. With an early start a garden can lay the foundations for an equable temper at twenty, a balanced judgment at forty, a

* See Appendix 1.
† See Appendix 2.

feeling of achievement at sixty and fulfilment at eighty. The wonder of childhood evolves into the serenity of old age.

'I knew you young, and love you now,
O shining grass, and shady bough.'
William Barnes, *Rustic childhood.*

By learning early on to entrust his spirit to nature as a swimmer learns to entrust his body to the water, a child finds the path to wisdom, for nature is God's creation.

★ ★ ★

The hidden order of nature is what I look for in a garden. Like the order that regulates the spire of Salisbury Cathedral, it may be studied in three different ways – scientific, aesthetic, and spiritual. That science must combine with nature to make a healthy garden goes without saying. Aesthetically we hope that the garden will give pleasure, or rather the multitude of pleasures of which this art form is capable. And spiritually another way of saying that the garden should reflect the order that lies at the heart of nature – not the molecular order that science measures, nor the order of beauty that students of aesthetics study, but the spiritual order – is that it should express the soul of its creator. For this spiritual order binds all living creatures. We share a common origin and we look to a common destiny in the universe.

What Maggie Keswick[3] has said of Chinese gardens is equally true of the mystic garden: 'It is easy to see why a Chinese garden might be thought of as a superior kind of religious experience.'

When I look at a garden, I see it as in transition. It is forever moving towards an ideal. In reality it can never reach completion. Plants die from injury or disease, or they have to be thinned out or transplanted. A garden that appears to be complete, with an air at once unchanging and unalterable, has ceased to give the impression of living; though its plants are alive, its soul is dead; so that as living creatures ourselves we cannot feel any kind of sympathy with it.* And though the ideal garden has no existence, it does have meaning for the imagination. This in itself is a human reality: just as two people in love believe they present, each to the other, and believe they see, each in the other, their real self, what actually passes between them is an ideal image, an image conjured up from the imagination to act as a stimulus towards perfection.

* One reason why a garden should be deliberately left unfinished in some detail is so that a visitor can complete it in his own imagination. Thus he is drawn into the garden, and as he reshapes it in his mind's eye so in turn the garden imposes its rule on him. He is stimulated to create the garden, not merely to observe it. The relation is dynamic, not passive.

CHAPTER FOUR

Expectation and Invitation

WE have seen how at Castle Drogo the entrance to the garden through a dark avenue of beeches reduces the sensory stimulation to which we are ordinarily subject. We see little except the light at the end of the tunnel; such sounds as we hear quieten the imagination rather than distract it, for a breeze rustling the leaves is all that vies with our footfall as we mount the steps, and, if there is anything of a wind blowing across from Dartmoor, the avenue breaks its force and encloses us in a cordon of calm air.

One of the historically earliest gardens to offer this experience was the small park designed by William Kent at Rousham (Oxfordshire) in about 1730 and still well preserved. It was one of the earliest too to be laid out entirely separately from the house and invisible from it, instead of being an architecturally concordant extension of it.

As at Castle Drogo, the visitor to Rousham's Vale of Venus enters the park by a path that goes down into the Vale through a tunnel of trees and shrubs. But the conclusion of this journey is different. Instead of being suddenly confronted by that startling view of the whole garden that Drogo offers, the visitor treading his way down to the Vale of Venus catches glimpses of it through the thinning shrubbery as the path descends. In the shade we feel nature take over. Leaves, branches, tree trunks and glimpses through them of the sky – all enclose our senses and sever the outer world from them. As we walk on we find that our mental images, the preconceptions and the suppositions, are all gradually extinguished, but then, as the shrubs thin out, stonework, statues, and ponds become visible through the branches. And, even though we may have seen them before, we find they are always different, varying with the season, the time of day, the weather, varying too in relation to the memories we already have of them; those memories from previous visits stored in a certain perspective, now undergo a change by the addition of another sight of them. Our *expectation* is aroused.

Descending into the Vale, we enter the world of classical Rome as conceived by the English travellers who made the Grand Tour of Europe in the eighteenth century and there learnt to love the Italian campagna. Up a grass slope to our right stands a pavilion known as the Praeneste. Designed by Kent in his typical style, it is intended to recall the ruined Temple of Fortune at Praeneste, now Palestrina, 25 miles (40km) east of Rome, which was much visited by travellers of the day. From the shelter of this building we can look down over the park and across a stream (the River Cherwell) to meadows where sheep are grazing. Far away on a low ridge stands an 'eye catcher' arch, a folly much in accordance with eighteenth century fashion, which draws the visitor's gaze away from the confines of the park to the expanses of a far horizon, and mingles his dream of the Italian campagna with the reality of the English countryside. To our left, in the Vale itself, are ponds and cascades or their dried up remnants, and statuary both Romano-Italian (a copy of the Medici Venus) and eighteenth century in inspiration.[1]

The whole park – and it includes many other delightful features – is much more than a place whose classical associations stirred the memory and the imagination of travellers who had done the Grand Tour or who had simply been educated in a society where everyone dipped into classical allusions daily. The park's setting in the rolling, farmed countryside of the English Midlands, and the manner in which carefully contrived views of this countryside form part of its design, indicate that, far from being a representation of an Italian scene, it symbolised a dream-like Elysium in the heart of England. In a loved but workaday countryside the park inspired in the minds of its visitors a vision of nature in harmony with itself and man, drawing the joys of innocence partly from the vanished life of an antique land, partly from the delights of travelling on holiday, and partly from the peaceful grazing of sheep in English meadows. To give substance to this vision, nature herself under Kent's handling has added the pleasures of shady woodland through which the sunlight falls in shafts, a sinuous rill, and grassy walks and groves.

At Stourhead (Wiltshire), created by the Hoare family over several generations in the eighteenth century, the park as at Rousham is separate from the house and the entrance is essentially similar. (Unfortunately, as at Drogo, the layout of the car park, shops, and so on diverts many visitors on to a backward course through the garden.) The path enters an increasingly darkening tunnel of trees and shrubs, until on the right appears a long vista leading up to an obelisk (nineteenth century replacement of an eighteenth century structure). The obelisk is sited far enough away for it not to tempt us to stray from the main path into the garden, and we continue on the path for a few paces to reach a viewpoint so striking that our footsteps are, literally, arrested. Of this, more below.

The path leads us in a gentle zig-zag down a wooded hillside, where, through the tree trunks and low shrubs, we see spread out the lake, the wooded hills opposite, and near the water's edge the Pantheon (or Temple of Hercules) designed by Henry Flitcroft as a miniature version of the Pantheon in Rome (now a church and mausoleum) and strongly resembling a temple in the painting by Claude Lorraine of the 'Coast View of Delos with Aeneas,' now in the National Gallery, London.

The beauty of the scene that awaits our enjoyment appears in premonitory and ever changing glimpses through the trees as we wind our way down the hillside towards the lake. As at Rousham our expectation is heightened by these intimations. Moment by moment the view changes as the tree trunks disclose first one and then another part of the picture we are about to enter. Expectation is followed by a sense of elation as we approach the lakeside, and we hurry to greet it or dawdle to savour it as the mood takes us – travelling always by an indirect course as eighteenth century principles prescribed.

★ ★ ★

Attracting our steps towards a beautiful building or scene in a garden by means of a series of glimpses between trees and shrubs arouses a feeling of expectancy. Another method of doing this, popular from early medieval times (to judge from illustrations in manuscripts), is to frame a scene in an aperture in a wall or hedge. Far more attractively patterned and fretted 'windows' of this kind abounded in the great gardens of China than we have ever seen in the west,[2] partly because, while the Chinese partitioned their gardens into rooms by means of walls and buildings, we more often used hedges of yew, box, and beech for the same purpose. A peach-shaped window which adorns a wall would be impossible to cut into a hedge without an appearance of ludicrous contrivance.

'Stourton Church framed by the shrubs' (p. 29): Stourhead.

'The Temple of Apollo faces us on a hill opposite' (p. 29): Stourhead.

A particularly unusual example of a framed view, or rather two views side by side, is to be seen at Stourhead. On taking the path into the garden and passing the obelisk on our right (but before we reach the succession of views through the trees across to the Pantheon over the lake), we come to the viewpoint mentioned above. Here two apertures in the walls of shrubs and trees present to us contrasting prospects. On the left we look far down into the valley and see Stourton Church framed by the shrubs. Ahead through another window the Temple of Apollo faces us on a hill opposite.

What is really a composite picture to be viewed from the one point on the path is made up of such strangely discordant elements as to deserve applause from the Surrealists. The mediaeval church down in the vale, secluded and almost private, a focus of a living faith, an emblem of our civilisation and in itself sacred, is unconcerned about the proud temple of Apollo shining in the sun on the hilltop opposite. Two religions, cultures, philosophies of nature and of man's place in the universe are set before us as a prelude to our entering the great garden that lies ahead of us. Bethlehem and Delphi gaze across at each other here. Two ages of faith were brought together in the Age of Reason.

★ ★ ★

When considering the framing of a view in a garden it is worth devoting some thought to the framing of pictures. Our first object is to isolate the picture from adjacent pictures or other decorations, so that it has a boundary that clearly marks it out as requiring separate attention from its surroundings (conversely, some interior decorators advise their clients to leave a picture, especially a modern one, unframed precisely because they view the picture not for itself but as part of the decorative scheme). And then as well as isolating the picture we want to embellish it. So we choose a frame that goes well with that particular picture and increases its impact on the view by bringing out perhaps its grandeur, its severity, its tenderness, its antiquity, or its spirituality.

In addition the framing of a picture offers something metaphorically to the viewer that the framing of a garden view offers literally, and that is an *invitation* to step into the scene. Part of our response to a picture is muscular, especially when we are looking at a landscape or an interior that makes us feel we should like to step into it. We feel a tightening of different groups of muscles in turn as we contemplate a road winding round a lake, a path wending through the woods, the steps up a rock outcrop, or the slopes of a distant hillside meeting the sky in a painting by, say, Claude or Turner. Part of our enjoyment of the picture comes from physically entering the scene, walking sedately here, running eagerly there, pausing in the shade of trees for a picnic or beneath an overhanging crag for amorous dalliance. Barely perceptibly our muscles and hormones respond to the scene: physiological reaction and aesthetic appreciation are parts of the same response, so that in some degree both mind and body are moulded by that release of joy that great art accomplishes.

So in a garden. We see a part of it attractively presented through a window of wall or hedge and are beckoned to find our way to it. Good framed views are to be found in the gardens at Athelhampton (Dorset), Polesden Lacey (Surrey), and Bickleigh Castle (Devon), to name only a few.

Framed views excite our hopes that the area of garden we cannot see from where we are standing is all as beautiful as the fragment that the window shows us.

'The natural flights of the human mind are not from pleasure to pleasure, but from hope to hope.'

Samuel Johnson, *The Rambler*, No. 2.

The aim of the mystic garden must be to extend an invitation which, when accepted, translates hope into pleasure.

CHAPTER FIVE

Surprise

ONE of the more attractive intellectual pleasures is to be surprised. And garden designers have long realised that to surprise a visitor is to capture his interest in the garden and thus to lead him onwards to seek out its treasures. Hence the provision of 'windows' in walls and hedges, discussed above, to frame a view which catches our eye and provides a surprising contrast to the scene outside the frame where we are standing. Though it beckons to us in its frame, the view is not instantly accessible; in fact we wonder how to reach it and are encouraged to see how we may get to it. The contriving of an indirect approach to a feature of the garden glimpsed more directly was a cardinal necessity in eighteenth century design. Here is William Shenstone[1] writing on it:

'When a building, or other object has been viewed from its proper point, the foot should never travel to it by the same path, which the eye has travelled over before. Lose the object, and draw nigh, obliquely'.

But surprise can be overdone. In the early part of the nineteenth century it became a foible of the Picturesque school that Thomas Love Peacock[2] neatly ridiculed in his novel *Headlong Hall*, published in 1815:

'"Allow me," said Mr. Gale (who, with Mr. Treacle, was a very profound critic from Edinburgh), "I distinguish the picturesque and the beautiful and add to them, in the laying out of grounds, a third and distinct character, which I call unexpectedness.*" "Pray, sir," said Mr. Milestone, "by what name do you distinguish this character when a person walks round the grounds for a second time?"'*

Changes in our cultural civilities have at least removed from our gardens the waterworks which in many Renaissance gardens were suddenly turned on to deluge the unsuspecting visitor from a concealed fountain. Yet, despite a breath of fresh air from Mr Milestone (a character based on Repton, with a touch of Lancelot Brown), devices to arouse surprise by the most trivial trompe l'oeil have continued to be popular throughout the twentieth century. Among them are plane mirrors that appear to extend the garden through an archway, paths giving a false perspective by being gradually narrowed towards the further end, and urns of a size contrary to expectation as at Sutton Place (Surrey).

But to return to Mr Milestone's question, 'by what name do you distinguish this character when a person walks round the grounds for a second time?': I would suggest that we hope to inspire in that person not surprise but something of more lasting value, namely pleasurable expectation. Consequently, whatever prospect is presented in a surprising manner needs to be of sufficient beauty and interest to arouse that feeling on the second and subsequent visits.

A fine example of this principle is the garden at Mapperton (Dorset). Here the visitor walks on to the lawn beside the house, which is on his right, and looks across the smooth grass to meadows on the hillside beyond, where cattle graze and some clumps of trees meet the sky. But as he walks across the lawn a remarkable sight appears at his feet, for he soon finds himself looking down into a narrow valley containing a seventeenth–eighteenth century formal garden with fine statues, formal flower beds, clipped yews, rectangular ponds, and a later orangery – the whole concealed till he approaches the valley's rim at the edge of the lawn. So charming is this scene, so remote and otherworldly in its contrast to the lawn and meadows beyond, that the surprise at first encountering it gives way to pleasurable expectation on every subsequent visit.

Similar, but not quite so jewel-like in its setting, is the garden at Upton House (Warwickshire). Here we look across the lawn from the terrace of the house to a ridge opposite, where the horizon meets the sky. As we walk across the lawn a considerable valley opens at our feet, wherein terraced gardens can be entered from flights of steps in the hillside. As at Mapperton we are startled by the apparition of this garden on the first visit, and when we go there again our expectation of seeing the valley garden impels us to walk eagerly towards its edge and peer over.

Another source of surprise, perhaps too little considered in gardens, is deliberate *contrast*, not the contrived tricks of the advertising agent but the kind of contrast that beautifies nature itself. Lord Kames, eighteenth century Scottish judge and philosopher, declared[3] that:

'grandeur ought to be contrasted with neatness, regularity with wildness, and gaiety with melancholy, so as that each emotion may succeed its opposite: . . . we have nature for our guide, which in her most beautiful landscapes often intermixes rugged rocks, dirty marshes, and barren stony heaths.' ★

★ ★ ★

As we find our way, which is nature's way, into the secrets of a mystic garden, surprise and expectation have an important role in keeping us alert to the world of nature about us. For one thing, nature herself is full of surprises, so there is nothing unnatural in a garden that presents nature in such a way as to excite our attention, provided the surprise is not just a fashionable toy to be admired or smiled at once, but is on the contrary transformed into pleasurable expectation on subsequent visits.

Furthermore, the contemplative state, the losing of self in nature's world, is capable of degenerating into undirected musing if we are not kept alert. The ennui, or accidie, the spiritual torpor that traditionally was apt to ensnare monks and nuns, needs to be guarded against also on a spiritual journey in the mystic garden. And what better antidote to it than the shock of surprise when coming upon a scene for the first time, or the tingling of expectation we feel on subsequent occasions as we hurry towards a remembered pleasure?

But any attempt to seize our attention by clever trickery or to impress us with rich ornamentation or fashionable osten-

★ See Appendix 3.

tation will simply cause embarrassment rather than induce reverence. Certainly the first sight of a garden should arouse curiosity and wonder, but to touch our heart effectively the good gardener acts discreetly.

'Wealth and place breed insolence
That brings ruin in its train.
When your work is done, then withdraw!
Such is Heaven's Way.'

Tao Tê Ching, ch. 9.

* * *

Though artefacts may keep us alert with their ingenuity, a deeper undercurrent of expectation binds us more firmly to our own garden. We live for the future; dig, sow, weed, hoe, stake, and prune all for the future. We may stand and admire the garden for a few moments, but soon we start imagining what it ought to look like in a month's or a year's time. Expectation is what gives us the face of contentment as we work in it through sun and rain. We labour in accordance with the needs of the garden, and our life joins there with the life of nature. The garden has a future, and so have we.

CHAPTER SIX

Boundaries

IF any proof were needed of how garden visitors today disregard the great philosophical statements which we have inherited from the eighteenth century, we need look no further than their null response to the ha-ha. A particularly beautiful example of this device is at Killerton (Devon). On my many visits to that garden I have noticed the visitors scrutinising with minute attention, sometimes with notebook in hand, the plants in the fine herbaceous borders (attributed to William Robinson originally), or examining the tender shrubs and climbers growing against the house, or simply enjoying the drifts of cyclamen and daffodils on the grassy banks in spring. But few indeed ever pause to admire what I believe is the prime feature of the garden, and that is the view over the lawn to the park beyond. It is seen by walking up the sloping lawn to its western corner and then turning to look south. From that point we see the lawn falling away at our feet to the invisible line of the ha-ha, whose presence is evident only from a slight change in green hue from lawn to parkland. In the park itself are well arranged clumps of deciduous trees, mostly oaks, and the eye travels through them across a shallow valley to the ridge of Woodbury Common in the distance.

'We see the lawn falling away at our feet to the invisible line of the ha-ha' (p. 37): Killerton.

This ha-ha, which has been improved in recent years by the National Trust, is pre-eminent for the seamless continuity of the view down over the mown lawn through cultivated parkland, where sheep and cattle graze, to the line of hills melting into the sky. But more than that: it gives us a perfect example of what the Japanese call 'borrowed scenery.' This term does not simply mean a good view. The Japanese use it to denote the arrangement of the garden's trees and shrubs, the slope of the ground, and the lie of any river or lake it has, in a continuous perspective with the woods and hills and valleys beyond.[1] Thus the garden and the surrounding countryside are united in a single landscape. Furthermore, the implication of a *living* landscape underlies the use of the term. Hills and valleys, woods, lakes, rivers, and man-made buildings such as a church or a classical pavilion all may be brought into the picture, but in such a way that the result is an organic whole.

Another essential technique in the correct borrowing of scenery is 'trimming' – that is, by means of hedges, walls, shrubs, an artificial hill and other devices the scene is trimmed, as one might trim a photographic print, to eliminate unwanted and confusing features.[2] Lancelot Brown (1716–83) was skilled at placing belts of trees to conceal farmland or neighbouring estates, thereby giving identity to the enclosed park. Repton (1752–1818) provides many examples of this technique of selective blocking out of parts of the landscape by carefully placed clumps of trees or artificial grassy knolls in the proposals he set before his clients in the Red Books.

Though the theory of borrowed landscape is important in Japanese garden design, we in Britain are perfectly familiar with the practice. As examples we may see a borrowed hill at

'The spectacular ruins of Fountains Abbey' (p. 41): borrowed scenery at Studley Royal.

Powis Castle (Powys), a church at Arlington Court (Devon), the spectacular ruins of Fountains Abbey at Studley Royal (North Yorkshire), and, one of the most beautiful of all, an island in the sea (Thatcher Rock) framed by trees and shrubs in the public garden on the Marine Drive, Torquay.

The borrowing of scenery is very much part of the philosophy of the ha-ha, for nature is thereby brought into closer intimacy with culture. The growth of a romantic acceptance of nature from early in the eighteenth century, the expression of a need for closer contact with a nature that seemed to expand the imagination and enhance the sensibility, was expressed by the ha-ha's unification of the observer with the scene through the harmonious fitting together of the landscape in a continuous perspective.

Nor was it only nature's wild or sweet embrace that was sought, for another effect of the ha-ha is to extend our sense of space. From being bounded the landscape becomes limitless; from being restricted, circumscribed, oppressive even, it ranges across the ha-ha to the freedom of the woods and hills, to the glimpse of infinity at the horizon where the last ridge meets the sky. To meaner minds in the eighteenth century the extension of space was little more than a display of personal aggrandisement, but to most people then and since it has seemed to be a noble expression of, at the lowest, civic liberty, and at a higher level the soaring of the human spirit.

'Space, like time, engenders forgetfulness; but it does so by setting us bodily free from our surroundings and giving us back our primitive, unattached state.'

Thomas Mann, *The Magic Mountain.*

Now, sad to say, the grand vista in which man's soul could find refreshment in the eighteenth century is everywhere in Britain much shrunken. The population has increased five-fold, and at every turn the eye falls on a new factory or office block, business park, service area, or housing estate, while the farmers fill their land with steel barns and silos. Great landowners may no longer sweep a village away to get a clear view of the distant hills at, sometimes, a shameful cost in human misery, but today's motorways cut their swathes through towns, villages, houses, historic landscapes, havens of wildlife, sites of special scientific interest, and National Parks.

'Ill fares the land, to hast'ning ills a prey,
Where wealth accumulates, and men decay.'
Oliver Goldsmith, *The Deserted Village.*

No wonder that the special virtues of the ha-ha go unregarded. Urban sprawl has driven us back to a modern version of the *hortus conclusus* from which the broad acres of the eighteenth century, and the acceptance of nature as benign rather than threatening, had allowed men to break free. What we have come to expect now are walls, fences, hedges, shrubberies – a refuge among partitions: all have grown up to protect us, not from a wilderness as in ancient times, but from our neighbours. Space has given way to privacy, the garden with enticing vistas to the garden with secluded rooms.

* * *

In a thought-provoking book Professor Jay Appleton[3] describes his theory of prospect-refuge symbolism. He applies it to natural landscapes and to man-made gardens, to urban landscapes, to paintings and photographs, and to literary descriptions. By a prospect he means any feature, object or situation which directly facilitates observation or indirectly suggests an opportunity to extend the field of vision. An example of prospect symbolism in a garden would be the distant view obtainable over a ha-ha or through a *clair-voie* in a hedge or from the summit of a mount. By contrast, in the category of refuge he includes anything which actually affords, or symbolically suggests, an opportunity to hide or shelter. The *hortus conclusus* would seem to fit this description perfectly, and the many gardens popular today that are divided into 'rooms' between hedges may be seen likewise as symbols of refuge.

This dichotomy can be applied to almost any feature of the environment, and Appleton does indeed take it into all sorts of situations. The division is not presented as hard-and-fast; there are degrees of prospect and refuge, and both may exist in different parts of the same landscape or picture. What is of special interest here is the source of this dichotomous strategy in the human mind. Appleton attributes it to the *desire to see without being seen* that must have had an important role in enabling primitive man to survive in the competition for food and territory. And we, the modern descendants of those distant hunting ancestors, have inherited in our cultural attitudes traces of a strategy, now applied to different ends, of what to them was a powerful necessity. The imperative that governed our ancestors' lives has been transformed into one of the bases of our own aesthetic pleasure.

There is scope here for a scientific investigation of the thesis. But surely without that it may be thought acceptable within certain limits. One of these seems to me to be that the theory itself, though put forward as applying to mankind in general, has much less relevance in the orient than in the occident. It is very much a product of western thinking about primitive man. Certainly Appleton's discussion of prospect and refuge in relation to Japanese gardens seems strained. Though it is based in part on a book by a Japanese writer, the passage he quotes gives an idiosyncratic and incomplete account of Japanese gardens. Moreover, we need to bear in mind that our own responses in the west to views of the countryside, man-made landscapes and gardens, and works of art and literature are subject to many other mental attitudes – rational, emotional, spiritual – some of them perhaps established more deeply and determinedly than the prospect-refuge strategy.

★ ★ ★

From the earliest times a garden protected by a wall from the surrounding wilderness has appealed to man's desire for shelter and shade, for cool water, refreshment, and privacy. The *hortus conclusus* offered protection against the onslaughts of both nature and thieves. It is certainly the type of garden that has endured longest throughout history in the west. In twentieth century Britain it is as popular, though in modified forms, as ever it was in mediaeval and Tudor times, though now its main purpose is not to provide protection for its owners so much as a unification of their house and garden in a single living area. A well known contemporary designer,[4] John Brookes, gives us today's perspective when he tells us that

'A garden should work as an extension of the house both practically and visually.'

A hundred years ago another garden architect, Reginald Blomfield, uttered the same thought:[5]

'the formal garden will produce with the house a homogeneous result, which cannot be reached by either singly.'

Gardens of this kind lean on architectural and decorative skills rather than on nature, and they are often subject to the same kind of embellishment as a house owner would devote to his carpets and wallpapers. Yet at their best they are refreshing reminders that other life forms do exist somewhere beyond the tarmac. The house may dominate, but the hint is there of a natural world that can speak to us in a voice at once authentic and seductive.

While the popularity today of architectural gardens with a succession of hedged or walled rooms is partly due to the urban background of their owners, who feel more secure in an extension of the house into the garden than in an extension of nature into the garden, they have another appeal too. That is, the provision of shelter in the garden's various compartments for different kinds of plants. This is surely an admirable practice, unless it degenerates into housing a *collection.* Innumerable different species, varieties, and cultivars, without botanical or aesthetic significance, are arranged like so

'The provision of shelter in the garden's various compartments' (p. 45): Hidcote.

many stamps in an album to make up that contemporary horror, the 'plantsman's garden'.

The collecting instinct is one manifestation of the instinct for territorial possession which is widely distributed throughout the animal kingdom and deeply embedded in mankind. Since about 1800 it has been a notable governor of gardeners' behaviour, for plant hunting expeditions have greatly increased in number and range, and they have brought back many species which now adorn our gardens and greenhouses. Often financed by enthusiastic gardeners, the plant hunters would distribute their collections among their sponsors, and, as wealth accumulated, one business magnate vied with another to impress his friends – and indeed to their great enjoyment a much wider public – with the novelty and variety of the plants he possessed on his estate.

But apart from these laudable essays in botany and horticulture we have seen in the present century tropical forests stripped of rare orchids, New World deserts robbed of their cacti, Mediterranean hillsides denuded of bulbs, corms, and tubers, and the European mountains surreptitiously deprived of ferns and flowering alpine plants. 'What I brought home in my sponge-bag' represents an attitude that merges imperceptibly into the encouragement of an illicit trade that is ruining the natural environment with all too little protest from gardeners themselves. Incredibly too we now see gardeners, who normally would protest their honesty, stealing so many seeds, cuttings, and even whole plants from gardens they visit that the National Trust is seriously worried by the losses, and some of those owners who used to open their gardens to the public for charity have ceased to do so.

A true botanic garden is of course another thing altogether, a collection made on systematic principles to illustrate genetic relationships. There we have a guiding philosophy directed to understanding the mysteries of nature. By contrast the 'one of everything' garden fails to display any understanding of the relations between individual plants, and it debases the study of their nature by the emphasis invariably placed on 'rarity' – a favourite selling point in plant catalogues. For a striking feature of the natural environment is the intimacy with which each organism occupies a niche. In a garden, plants of the same species are suitably associated in clumps, or they may be dispersed if so placed that they seem to call to each other over the intervening ground. Three trees of the same kind, for instance, beckon to each other with a natural concordance that trees of different kinds would lack. The whole of nature makes a patterned cloth of life where each organism collaborates with its associates or pushes them out, establishes its progeny or loses them, withstands wind and rain and drought or succumbs to them. A mystic garden reflects in symbolic form something of these struggles.

★ ★ ★

Despite the unnatural character of architectural gardens as they have been developed over the last hundred years, and the urban minds that they reflect, they are nevertheless capable of inspiring a mystic contact with nature and in some ways are particularly well adapted to doing so. The isolation they impose in separating us off from distractions outside and the sense they give us of being alone with nature are conditions well suited to the initiation of mystical experience. Just as the entrance to a garden through a dark tunnel clears the mind and prepares it for 'rebirth' in the new world of the garden, so does a walled garden provide a shelter not only from the cold wind but, by suggestion, from our mundane worries too; it offers a tranquil refuge, while holding our energies fast within its confines. The enclosure compresses our imagination and prepares us for that leap into freedom, that flash of comprehension we feel as we enter into communion with the source of our being. The restriction of the senses imposed by the garden walls sets free a deeper consciousness of the world about us.

At its most intense this experience can wholly change a person's destiny. It can transform our character through the overthrow of established emotional responses, ways of thought, temperamental attitudes, and the direction in which we have been driving. A new consciousness sweeps the old life away and sets us on a course more expressive of our true self, and more in harmony with the way that beckons us on. I know this from personal experience. A landslide permanently alters the course of the river.

CHAPTER SEVEN

Joy and Mystery

TO a child a bright colour needs no meaning. In itself it is attractive whatever its source – whether a sweet, a dolls' dress, a string of beads, a rattle, a cushion, a flower. Nor is it only to children that brilliance of colour appeals. If that had been so, the Impressionists would have lived and died in vain. But we are conscious every time we go into a garden in Britain that for much of the year it is covered with grey skies. In summer drought or winter snow, in rain and frost and storm, the clouds are dense for days and weeks at a time. No wonder we crave for colour in the garden.

Generally speaking, I believe a small garden needs, in proportion to its size, more colour than a large one, because it lacks the scope for plants of interesting character and the space for variety of enchanting views that a greater area affords. Yet it is hampered in that, to obtain its colour, it cannot turn to that quintessentially English invention, the herbaceous border. Space, long and wide space, is needed for a herbaceous border that is to be a success for more than a few weeks in the summer. To have a display from the beginning of June to the end of September necessitates a careful choice of plants in relation to their normal flowering times quite apart from their colour, height, and any other qualities needed to make a well-balanced border. Too small a border, whether in length or width or both, allows too few varieties of plants to be grown to provide a succession of flowers. Hence the dull and bedraggled appearance in so many gardens of their small borders and 'island beds' during most months of the year.

The fact is that a border with herbaceous perennials, with some annuals and biennials to fill the gaps, is gardening not only at its most demanding, but also at its most fleeting: especially if the summer is dry, when the flowers soon wither (for watering is generally forbidden nowadays); or wet, when the plants are spreadeagled and their flowers shattered; or dull and cloudy, when growth is poor and flowering inhibited; or windy, when many stems keel over. Yet in a perfect summer, in just the right week, the gardener may feel exultant that all the work he has put into his floral display has reached a glorious climax.

One of the greatest exponents of using plants in the purely pictorial manner of the herbaceous border was Gertrude Jekyll, who was a painter and admirer of Turner's pictures until impaired vision turned her attention to devising planting schemes for clients who sought her advice on how to improve their gardens. Economic forces have made her plans generally impossible of fulfilment nowadays. A few gardens survive bearing witness to her ideas, but only in slight degree. At Hestercombe (Somerset), where she gave advice on the planting up of Lutyens's design, she devised a 'grey' garden, which has been faithfully restored, together with the rest of the garden, by the Somerset Fire Brigade, whose headquarters is there.

But it was at Barrington Court (also in Somerset), for long kept up by the Lyle family in accordance with her original principles, that the supreme contemporary example of her painter's eye for colour could be seen. (It has changed hands and is not now open to the public.). The beds and borders there were filled with a sumptuous, entrancing succession of flowers throughout the summer which in their gradation of hue or striking boldness beguiled the eye and ever led us on through the garden from each brilliant clump to the next. Or so it seemed in August 1981; but I never saw the garden look quite so good again on the several visits I paid it.

A great deal of skilled labour is needed to bring herbaceous beds and borders to perfection, yet in a poor summer the achievement may be all too evanescent. And the gardener ends by sighing the same regret as Tarquin uttered when in pursuit of Lucrece:

> *'What win I if I gain the thing I seek?*
> *A dream, a breath, a froth of fleeting joy.'*
>
> W. Shakespeare, *The Rape of Lucrece.*

In fact so many gardeners have shared Tarquin's qualms that, of the great herbaceous borders which earlier this century adorned innumerable gardens, few remain in anything like their original form. Shrubs have taken over from herbaceous plants, and the blaze of colour has faded. The labour needed for planting, splitting up, staking, tying in, cutting down, replacing, filling gaps, and dead heading is too expensive – and the joy too fleeting.

* * *

Beautiful as these floral gardens are, we should not pretend that they open our eyes to the secrets of nature. They bring us joy, but not enlightenment. They elate us with wonder at the gleaming surface, but there is nothing behind, no ulterior thought. And that is their charm. Confronted with a herbaceous border of the old style, we simply rejoice. We are in holiday mood. The *lacrimae rerum* fall elsewhere.

Yet a garden whose whole appeal lies in its floral display misses something, just as a garden that is beautiful only in sunshine lacks much that is moving in nature. Rain, wind, frost, snow – all bring out a different face whose beauty is in the character that responds to these trials.

★ ★ ★

But below the surface is a reality that most great painters have tried to reach and communicate, and some gardeners too. In the depths where we comprehend by symbol lies a truth about our existence that is only hinted at by the glancing of sunlight across leaves and petals. If a garden reflects the soul of its creator, it must in consequence convey something of the mystery of life.

Here we need to be clear that we are not confusing mystery with ignorance. Much of such knowledge as we have about the origin of life on earth and of how living creatures evolved is speculative, but Darwin and Mendel have been followed in the twentieth century by a host of workers in biology, chemistry, and population statistics who have laid bare many of what were formerly life's secrets, and that process will go on. This is one approach to the understanding of life's

'Rain, wind, frost, snow – all bring out a different face' (p. 53): Stourhead in driving rain.

mystery. Its validity is unchallenged but its scope is bounded by the rules within which it operates, the very restrictions that make it so effectual. In scientific terms it will be increasingly successful through observation, experiment, and independent testing.

But in that mystery too lies the meaning life has for each of us as individuals, and there science has no power to enter. It is as though a painting by Rembrandt were analysed physically and chemically down to the last flake of pigment and the last square millimetre of canvas to give us a complete scientific statement of its composition and manner of production. Theoretically such an analysis is possible. Yet of the picture's aesthetic effect on the viewer, its entire raison d'être, science can say nothing with any meaning. Nor can metaphysics.

'Pray make a firm resolution never to think of metaphysics. Speculations of that kind are absurd in a man, but in a woman are more absurd than I choose to express.'

James Boswell in a letter to
Belle de Zuylen on 9 July 1764.[1]

Who ever heard of a woman being a great metaphysician? They have too much common sense to go wandering off into the dream world of:

Metaphysics: 'theoretical philosophy of being and knowing' (*Concise Oxford Dictionary*); 'the science which investigates the first principles of nature and thought' (*Chambers Twentieth Century Dictionary*).

These discordant definitions from two respected sources – in the one it is a theoretical philosophy, in the other a science – are evidence enough of confusion in learned circles about what metaphysicians do. And recourse to their published works shows either that the conclusions they have reached cannot be tested or that the subjects they discussed have since become the objects of scientific inquiry. Boswell was right. Yet he was a questing and imaginative man, and his opinion of metaphysics did not stop him from speculating frequently on the meaning of our existence and whether we have the freedom of will to choose our destiny.

What he realised in a prescientific age is that the application of reason *in a theoretical context* to important problems of our being can never solve them. Only *direct experience*, which he tasted so intensely, could give the understanding of life that he sought. In its most intimate form such experience comes to a baby when he crawls across a lawn and receives a sensory impression of, for example, something hard, rough, and rounded (not of course that he thinks of his sensations in such terms) and has not yet learnt to coordinate the impressions and to classify them in the category of, say, a tree trunk.

'Banish wisdom, discard knowledge,
And the people will be benefited a hundredfold.'
Tao Tê Ching, ch. 19.

This injunction, which seems paradoxical to the western mind, means that by reverting to a child's direct, raw experience of the world we gain a fresh understanding of it; just as, on a visit for the first time to a foreign country, we see everything, even the most commonplace, with a wideawake wonder and our vision of it is intensified. And of deeper mysteries too Jesus said:

'I thank thee, O Father, Lord of heaven and earth, that thou hast hid these things from the wise and prudent, and hast revealed them unto babes.'

St Luke, 10, 21.

★ ★ ★

Children experience the mystery of a garden more sharply than adults do. They know the secret places in the shrubbery, or behind the bole of an old tree, or in the hollow of a bank curtained by hanging ivy. So in a mystic garden it is our childlike sense of wonder that is aroused, wonder at the variety and mystery of life. This is not necessarily its only or main purpose, but when we stand in the garden we should feel: *This is a magic place.* A naturalist studying a group of plants has the same feeling when he reaches a locality, not superficially very different from many others, where those plants are particularly richly represented. Life is specially varied or abundant there; species that are at the limit of their range, or are so dependent on rarely occurring conditions that they are found at few localities anywhere in the world, have their home there; and in such favoured places many other forms of life may abound too. The whole locality seems to be a magic cave of life. Knowing that there are historical, geographical, and ecological reasons why it should be so, the naturalist sets about trying to analyse them. But alongside his scientific study he feels, if he has any soul to do so, that the place in itself, with its peculiarly favourable habitat to the thriving of life, appeals to, not exactly his aesthetic sense, but rather his spiritual understanding of the richness of life.

We may experience the same understanding at the centre of our being when we sit in the silence of an old village church as the sun shines through the south aisle across pillars that have been leaning agley for centuries; or after a tramp over the wild moors when we come upon a megalithic stone circle, remote, fragmented, partly fallen, in a wide expanse of sky filled with the song of skylarks above the rustling grass.

★ ★ ★

The mystery of 'rebirth' that some gardens offer us as a prelude to stepping into the new world at the end of the tunnel was familiar enough to the eighteenth century landscapists, as they showed in the entrances to such gardens as Rousham and Stourhead. But their representation of nature's mystery went further, permeating their gardens in a variety of ways. Like life itself the garden stored memories of an earlier, more natural, existence before man became self-conscious. And it showed him a way through present time that guided him from a past where his roots lay to a future where he might attain fulfilment. The paths and rides were sinuous not only because Hogarth's 'line of beauty' was curved, as a reflection of feminine beauty, but to reveal to the visitor a succession of unexpected vistas as he walked or rode over them. And clumps of trees, grassy hillocks, lines of shrubs, or a shoulder of a hillside concealed the future, blocking the visitor's direct way and forcing him to go round and about. Again, in their treatment of lakes they disclosed the real extent of the water only gradually. Lancelot (Capability) Brown in particular was famous for his skill in concealing the end of a lake from view at the main vantage points, so that the imagination was free to play on its possible course round the curve of the shore.

The curve of a garden path should not be fussy or acutely irregular. Nor should its course be bland or lacking clear direction. Rather, taking a natural course, it should go round some object such as a tree or flowerbed with that object in its concavity, not standing outside the path's convexity. Here two kinds of sinuosity may be distinguished – the predictable and the unpredictable. A predictable curve is one that swings more or less equally each way in turn, like a sine curve representing alternating electric current, or one that diminishes in amplitude when representing the vibration of a musical note fading away. Such curves are commonly seen as ancient ways up hillsides, where for centuries man and horse have swung first this way and then that in trudging uphill through the mud. The toil and sweat of their struggle to reach the goal is now embalmed on many a hill in a tarred lane lined with a pair of hedges.

'On a huge hill,
Cragged and steep, Truth stands, and he that will
Reach her, about must and about must go,
And what the hill's suddenness resists, win so.'

John Donne, *Seek true religion!*

Nature is full of unpredictable curves also, when the walker has no idea which way his course will lie round the next bend.* Again, in the garden, though entirely permissible, the curves should not be such as to agitate the walker.

* See Appendix 4.

Artificial ornaments may too arouse us to touch the source of our being. An antique statue rough with lichen and moss, sheltered in an alcove among the trees, fastens our attention with its pensive or merry gaze and draws us into a distant past whose culture and beliefs we have inherited. Or a modern sculpture, perhaps of abstract form, stands among the ferns, where its flowing, organic lines shadowed by the passing sun call to mind the impulse of living things to undergo evolutionary change in unimagined directions in order to evade extinction.

* * *

Contemplating these mysteries of the garden we pause to ask. What is the meaning of all this richness and variety of tree and grass and flower, the meaning of the spirit that beckons to us from the darkness of a grove, from the brilliance of azaleas lining a path in spring, from the ivory petals of a water-lily flower, from the swaying of a fern frond? And the achievement of the mystic garden is that from it we learn to look for the answer within each of us. Though it is inexpressible in words, we discover it by living fully.

CHAPTER EIGHT

Perseverance

A mystic garden is not created in a few days from some ideas sketched out on a pad, or even in a few weeks from the plans drawn (perhaps with computer aid) by a professional designer. Several seasons are needed for it merely to take shape. And if it is to reflect the heart of nature and the quest of each of us to find that heart beating in our own, its creator is unlikely to entrust much of its design, if any, to another person except on purely technical questions such as drainage or the laying of paths.

> *'Great works are performed not by strength, but perseverance.'*
> Samuel Johnson, *The history of Rasselas, Prince of Abissinia.*

Examine all the gardens you wish before starting your own, but then forget them. Study the history of gardens and their aesthetic principles, visit the classic gardens of our own and earlier times, learn the science of good cultivation and the art of associating plants with each other. Look carefully at great paintings in art galleries, read poetry, listen to music. Then clear your mind of details. A framework will remain to help you give order to the inspiration you must now draw up from its depths. Far too many gardens are simply copies of other gardens, repeating the planting schemes of their contemporaries or reproducing patterns that had their origin in the cultures of past centuries. Topiary carvings in box which have no more originality than a flight of china ducks on a sitting-room wall are joined by knot gardens that imitate those of Tudor times, rockeries that tumbled out of Edwardian picture books, and 'white gardens' that miss the purpose of their original at Sissinghurst, which was an enclosure for Vita Sackville-West to pass through at night.

A deeply satisfying garden is years in the making, because the satisfaction it gives springs from the quality of the human spirit that is poured into it. Only over years of effort and the experience of both achievement and failure do we acquire a framework of true values and a clear understanding of our existence. Nor can this body of wisdom be imparted to the garden in a hurry as we make it in collaboration with nature.

The easy way is never nature's way. Filling a gap from the local garden centre without much thought is a temporary expedient. We all do it. But to run a garden permanently on those lines is to lose the way. To hold the secrets of nature a garden must grow from its creator's hands during the years of striving, pondering, experimenting, labouring, – yet like a great painting it speaks to us with effortless mastery.

'Perfect activity leaves no track behind it;
Perfect speech is like a jade-worker whose tool leaves no mark.'

Tao Tê Ching, ch. 27

* * *

The beauty of a cottage garden is often admired for its natural but pleasing mixture of fruit and vegetables and decorative plants in profusion, perhaps with roses and honeysuckle scrambling up the wall and almost burying the house in a jungle of sweetly scented vegetation. The whole confection is the product of striving over many years, sometimes several generations, to provide for the household's needs – both food and beauty – as economically as possible. For the essence of a cottage garden is that its plants are grown from seeds saved from last year's flowers or from cuttings exchanged among neighbours. Behind the picture of prolific life lie years of perseverance through rural poverty.

So I wince when I hear, as I so often have, a well-off gardener saying, 'My garden is really just a glorified cottage garden – that's the effect I aim at.' Such people have never thought to look behind the summer's riot in a true cottage garden at the labour and anxiety put into saving the seeds in autumn, germinating them in the kitchen window in spring, attacking the aphids with fingers dipped in soapy water, and trying to prevent the lettuces and cabbages from going to seed too soon.

A cottage garden touches the heart the more movingly when we understand the work its owner has put into it year after year with a skilled understanding of the needs of plants, from seed to fruit, that is unusual even among gardeners with a more sophisticated background. Here perhaps is a true mystic garden even though its owner might scorn to think so. He has put his heart and soul into it, and this is why such gardens have a special appeal to those of us who look for the symbol underlying the material scene and giving life to it.

Though cottage gardens have no history in the way a garden created round a great country house has, the ethos animating them does have a continuity of life and fertility running through them year after year. They are dedicated to self-sufficiency and kept going by the hands and backs and feet of their owners. Lacking anything so pretentious as a textbook design, they spread their natural way through the seasons, adapting, like a river flowing on to a flood plain, to each gap and each bare patch as it presents itself. In return for the love bestowed on them they yield food and flowers: a love which, like love in general, needs to be worked at with perseverance if it is to endure.

'The garden . . . stands for efficiency, for patience in labour, for strength in adversity, for the power to forgive.'

Sir George Sitwell.[1]

Nor is it only in the creation of a garden that perseverance is a virtue. In the understanding of it too, in grappling with its hidden message, we must fight off distracting influences while we enjoy the aesthetic satisfaction it offers, and continue our journey into the unknown. A garden should of course appeal to the eye, indeed to all the senses, but beyond whatever immediate response its beauty may arouse we should allow ourselves to be led onwards in our philosophic quest. After accepting its beauty we should also be induced to think how exciting, or peaceful, or puzzling the garden is, how reassuring, or provoking, or adventurous, or harmonious – and so it should impart to us some of those qualities that enhance our experience of life. Beauty is indispensable to our happiness, but alone it is not enough. The environment moulds our minds, while we in turn mould the environment. Thus a garden helps us to understand our destiny if we can only persevere in its creation year in year out, not until it is complete (for it never will be) but until it bears uniquely the impress of its creator's own nature.

'The works of a person that builds, begin immediately to decay; while those of him who plants begin directly to improve.'

William Shenstone.[2]

* * *

Just as ruins seemed in the past, according to Shenstone,[2] to 'afford that pleasing melancholy which proceeds from a reflexion on decayed magnificence,' so today we are more likely to respond in this way to the sight of a decayed old tree. Perhaps its main branches are propped up as though they were the limbs of an old man struggling with a crutch or walking-stick to defy the weakness that bears him down. Its hollow trunk suggests a body which has few channels left for the sap to course through. Yet the leafy twigs here and there show that the tree is still alive, an organism held together by its memories and still able to enforce its will to live.

Trees contorted by wind and frost over many years, perhaps centuries, express that mysterious will to survive that all living things have. In persevering and enduring they put into graphical form, as it were, the eternal striving of living creatures to reach maturity and reproduce their kind. Scientifically these impulses can be measured; aesthetically we admire the living symbol of the struggle; spiritually we take courage to continue on life's way. And further than that, for as Suzuki[3] has remarked: 'every old tree of any sort inspires a beholder with a mystic feeling which leads him to a faraway world of timeless eternity.'

Sadly, this thought may not be so readily accepted in the western world today as in the orient or as it would have been in the Graeco-Roman civilisations. A feature of our age is the 'information explosion'. Huge quantities of facts are available at the touch of a computer key; they may not be true, but they pour on to the screen in profusion. Yet what we need is not more facts but more wisdom. Only living intensely can give that. A young person has not had time to acquire wisdom. An old person has had the opportunity, but has he had the will to do so? Experience, perception, endurance: an old tree has learnt to bend in the wind, an old man to take what comes. That is the course the gardener learns to follow.

CHAPTER NINE

Knowledge

SEEING directly into the human condition is something artists help us to do through their paintings, music, poetry, and drama, and from a different approach sacred texts and rituals lead us to an intuitive understanding of our relationship with the universe. Likewise a mystic garden breathes life into us as we seek below the surface for the meaning it holds in its green shade. What a mystic garden – or any garden – should teach us above all is reverence: reverence for people, for plants and animals, for all of nature, including rocks, water, earth, rain streaming over the leaves, snow folded like white velvet over the mounds of shrubs.

Though intuition and contemplation take us into the hidden meaning of the garden, we should not ignore the help we can get from plain intellectual work. Whatever the course of our quest to reach the heart of life's secret, whether it leads us through realms of art, or religion, or nature, some factual knowledge helps to orientate us and to prevent our imagination from straying into attractive but misleading byways. Intellectual study and factual knowledge are insufficient in themselves to lead us far along the way. The raw, naked experience of children will take them far, as noted above. But, when we cease to be children and our minds have acquired a strong intellectual framework, we can make good use of that framework before we let it slip into abeyance as intuitive understanding takes over.

In studying a painting, for instance, we appreciate its particular artistry more fully if we know when the artist lived, where he painted it (Paris? London? Venice?), what he depicts in it, perhaps how old he was at the time and what earlier masters had influenced him. I am not suggesting the ordinary lover of art needs anything more than a general knowledge of the painting's context; the details are for art historians, critics, students of the era, and theologians if a religious painting is in question. But to enjoy a painting with the greatest intensity of delight we are greatly helped if we can amplify our first response, whether pleasurable or startled, by having our interest coordinated with the outlook of the artist and his contemporaries. This is particularly true of that art in which mystic symbolism is of special significance, namely the vast assemblage of Christian paintings and sculpture that lie at the centre of western art; and it is no less true of the religious art of the east.

Likewise with gardens. The journey below the surface to reach the symbol is essentially intuitive, but we start on the way with a much surer step if we have some factual knowledge of the context in which the garden was created. Garden history is a study that has expanded out of all recognition since about 1950, and more recently it has been joined by garden archaeology. Owing to work done by scholars in these subjects we can now examine many gardens in Britain and western Europe with a clearer understanding of what they meant to their contemporaries than was formerly possible. This is of especial value to our attempt to get below surface appearances in gardens made from about 1700 to 1830, when gardens were often deliberately endowed with a symbolic significance that drew its inspiration from the philosophical outlook of the time.

As plutocracy expanded, philosophy faded. So that today, when the idea that a garden could have a philosophical or symbolic foundation is generally scorned, we may particularly value some knowledge of the history, literature, horticulture, and philosophy that may have influenced the making of a garden. Having mastered that, we set it aside and submit to the experience of the garden itself. To rejoice in our ignorance is debilitating. We need to study a map before starting our journey.

But after we have learnt, the time comes for us to forget. Let the learning mould our thought and imagination; then shed the received opinions so that our experience of the garden may be like the wonderment of a child, a direct interchange of life with life. It is not the past of our finest gardens that is their treasure but the beauty they offer us today; they are not historical monuments but unique works of art. Whether great art – a painting, a sculpture, a garden – has a history is of ancillary, technical interest only, and the greater the quality of the art the less important is the history. A masterpiece has no history that matters.

* * *

Where a garden stands in specific contrast to works of art or sacred texts is that it is composed of living organisms. Nor in an important respect are they part of our own lives. Each species has a different average life span characteristic of that species and so lives in a different time scale. An oak tree, for example, which may live for several hundred years, responds at a far more stately pace to the passage of time than a groundsel, which may live only a couple of months. Thus simply owing to their particular life spans the experience of life is entirely different for the primrose, which may expect to last a few years at most; a royal fern, which may outlive most men; or a lichen on a rock, which may reach a crusty old age of over a thousand years.

Accustomed as we are to thinking without question of the flow of time in the context of our own lives, we have to learn to think, as gardeners, of the very variable life spans of the plants in our care. We categorise them broadly as annuals, biennials, and perennials, and plan the growing of our plants in accordance with their speed of maturation. So in a garden there is an intricate web of time scales affecting the competition plants exert against each other, their rate of reproduction, their season of fruiting: time is a dimension affecting differently every kind of plant, and their times vibrate in us with varying harmonies. A garden full of annuals, for instance, disturbs us with its transience and restlessness. In contrast, mosses and lichens impart to an old statue of Pan or to trees and undisturbed banks an air of a long settled past, of permanency even, that promises to carry us with it into a tranquil future.

Of all the ornaments that adorn gardens I think the least

appropriate is a sundial, for it intrudes into the natural mixture of times an arbitrary and alien scale of man's invention.

> *'The hours of folly are measur'd by the clock; but of wisdom, no clock can measure.'*
>
> William Blake, *Marriage of Heaven and Hell.*

In learning to understand the relativity of time in the garden and of our own time in relation to it we come closer to appreciating the variety of nature and of understanding how nature perceives itself. The perception of living that a plant has is not of course conscious, but it is discernible physiologically in the way it responds to environmental pressures within its time scale: an annual plant hurrying into flower in hot, dry weather; a shrub coming into leaf after a heavy shower of rain; a tree dying several years after a drought has fatally impaired its roots.

But 'perception' is too anthropocentric a word. Though the whole manner of a plant's existence is governed by its specific time scale and the life span that is part of its nature, the feature of plants' lives that must especially strike us is that they cannot be in the least conscious of time. We are entering the myth of the Garden of Eden before the Fall. Time then had no meaning. With the loss of their innocence our progenitors became conscious not only of themselves as people but of their existence in time, as individuals in history. So in the mystic garden, where we look for an understanding of nature, including the nature of ourselves, we learn of existence in many time scales. Different epochs come together in the garden. As we wander through it, the scents of mown grass, sweet peas, old roses, onions, a clump of stocks, an autumn bonfire – any of them may draw up from the deeper layers of the mind memories of other days. The speculation of adolescence mingles with the confidence of middle life, the open wonder of infancy with the wisdom of old age. And our task is to break through the individual scales into the still centre beyond them, the centre no longer of innocence but of perfect understanding.

★ ★ ★

'There is a provinciality in time as well as in space. To feel ill-at-ease and out of place except in one's own period is to be provincial in time. But he who has learned to look at life through the eyes in turn of Chaucer, of Donne, of Pope and of Thomas Hardy is freed from this limitation. He has become a cosmopolitan of the ages, and can regard his own period with the detachment which is a necessary foundation of wisdom.'

Lord David Cecil.[1]

In the eighteenth century many of the great parks were adorned with pavilions, statues, busts, bridges, and inscribed plaques that recalled to their owner, and likewise to his cultured visitors, episodes from the literature of classical Greece and Rome. Anyone called to admire the scene was presumed to have the background knowledge with which to interpret the allusions to myth and legend suggested by it. Nor did the great landowners stop at myths and legends from classical times. Stowe is an example of a much wider field of reference.

Sir Richard Temple began in the 1680s to lay out the grounds in a rather formal manner; his son Sir Richard, later

Viscount Cobham, enlarged the landscape and introduced many naturalistic features; his nephew Earl Temple continued to elaborate the park and its buildings; and finally his nephew, the Marquess of Buckingham, added the last touches.[2] During this century of construction most of the leading landscapists of the day took a hand in designing the park. Yet despite the length of time over which this park was created and despite the succession of owners, it stands today as a glorious landscape which, though still crammed with a variety of temples and statues, together with its perfect Palladian bridge, breathes an air remarkable for the homogeneity of its philosophy and for the assurance with which the Temple family expressed their particular view of liberty, political as well as personal.

Strange as it may seem to us now, the French geometric gardens of an earlier generation, such as Le Nôtre's *tours de force* at Versailles and at Nicolas Fouquet's Vaux-le-Vicomte, shared with the English landscape parks the same objective. That was to disregard the accidental, superficial irregularities of nature in order to lay bare the underlying ideal form, nature in a state of perfection.

A garden designed in the geometric style of the seventeenth century in France could be observed in its entirety – or at least most of what mattered – from a single viewpoint. Often enough too its whole pattern could be deduced from examining quite a small section of it. From that the picture could be completed by repetition, duplication, extension, and inversion.★ In contrast a visitor to an English landscape garden

★ *'Grove nods at grove, each Alley has a brother,*
And half the platform just reflects the other.'
Alexander Pope, *Epistle to Burlington*.

needed to walk (or ride) for several hours over wooded paths and grassy banks to enjoy its variety of scenery; he might stand on a hillock and gaze over the lake or pause to lean over the parapet of a bridge to admire the curving away of the water; reaching a Graeco-Roman temple he might sit down on the steps and reflect on the ordered liberty enjoyed in Augustan Rome and Sir Robert Walpole's England; or sighting an ivy-covered ruin, genuine or manufactured, he might shed a tear over the transience of all man's achievements.

The idealisation of nature in terms of ordered patterns was entirely in accord with the considered opinion of René Descartes (1596–1650) that animals have no feelings; they are simply automata. Translated into the garden, his philosophy had no concern with the individuality of plants. But they had a use: and that was, severally and collectively, to serve as points and lines, circles and parabolas, here trimmed to form a straight allée through the untidy woodland, there carved into arabesques that could as easily have been made with coloured stones – and sometimes were.

Living at a time of growing political tolerance that was the practical expression in statecraft of the philosophical liberalism propounded by John Locke (1632–1704), the great landowners in England were conscious of enjoying a degree of freedom in an ordered society that inspired them to see nature as, below the rough surface, an Elysium, a Garden of Eden, where life was innocent of malice, envy, strife, and deceit, and regulated by good sense.

Indeed these two types of garden, the French and the English, closely reflected the minds of the statesmen and philosophers who influenced the outlook of their creators. The *'jardin anglais'* subsequently found some favour on the Continent, and the French geometric style after being ousted from England early in the eighteenth century returned occasionally later on to please a few adherents. (A notable example is the water parterre at Blenheim (Oxon) made in the 1920s by the French designer Achille Duchêne.) But the appeal of this cultural transplantation has never been more than marginal.

In the abundance and intricacy of its symbolic allusions Stowe stood alone, though many other parks had their walks and vistas planned round classical temples to transport the viewer to a legendary world to which the Age of Reason felt itself to be akin. But in deference not so much to the realities of the neighbouring countryside as to the landowner's romantic dreams the park often included a rustic bridge or gothic hut to remind him of nature's rougher face. Among those parks now vanished William Shenstone's The Leasowes must have been the most thought-provoking owing to his use of plaques bearing literary quotations to supplement the sculptural adornments. Of those that survive today, Stourhead and West Wycombe still give a uniquely penetrating glimpse of innocence and tranquillity. To leave one of these parks after walking round it is to wake from a dream calm and refreshed. The visitor retires with his perplexities smoothed away and his confidence restored,

'For he on honey dew hath fed,
And drunk the milk of Paradise.'

S. T. Coleridge, *Kubla Khan*.

* * *

'A uniquely penetrating glimpse of innocence and tranquillity' (p. 75): West Wycombe Park.

Though a full understanding of these parks requires of us today a knowledge of the many allusions their buildings and sculptures convey, that knowledge was bred into our eighteenth century forebears at home and at school. It permeated their literature and embellished their conversation; even at play their impersonations, conundrums, and spontaneous verses were filled with the gods of a golden age. What we think of as knowledge that today only an unusually cultivated person has acquired was then so deeply embedded as to be the common experience. Apart from Stowe, which was always something of a political acrostic, these parks, with their symbolic context, stimulated not the reason so much as the imagination. They gave their visitors the direct experience of nature in a civilised framework, not an exercise requiring interpretation.

This is where the limits of knowledge become apparent. A philosophic garden such as Stowe needed even in its own day some rational exposition if it was to make its full impact on the visitor. But a mystic garden appeals to direct experience. The appeal may be the more effective for a small degree of interpretation, but essentially the garden that responds to a mystic appeal arouses a different kind of understanding, intuitive beyond the limits of reason, touching the realm of love.

'Love will never come to an end. Prophecies will cease; tongues of ecstasy will fall silent; knowledge will vanish. *For our knowledge and our prophecy alike are partial, and the partial vanishes when wholeness comes.'*

St Paul, *I Corinthians 13, 8–10: (Revised English Bible).*

CHAPTER TEN

Finding the Way

TO enter into the spirit of a work of art, or to take part in a religious ritual, we need to hold in suspension, at least initially, any doubts we may have about the experience we intend to undergo. Later we may come to examine it more critically, but unless we begin by submitting to it we shall receive nothing from it.

'But as it is necessary not to invite robbery by supineness, so it is our duty not to suppress tenderness by suspicion; it is better to suffer wrong than to do it, and happier to be sometimes cheated than not to trust.'

Samuel Johnson, *Rambler*, No. 79.

Submission reaches to the heart of any experience. Conquest shuts us out from it. These words should not be given a political interpretation. Though pacific in intent, they would be misunderstood if taken to be a plea for pacifism in the military sense, for resistance to evil may be necessary if any good is to survive. But when we are seeking an intuitive understanding of life's mystery, whether in a garden or in a church, we must pursue our search for it – certainly with an open mind – but, more to the point and more difficult of attainment, with an open heart. Doubts, hesitations, critical comparisons, fashionable preconceptions – all these must be set aside. Ardour, revulsion, alarm, sentimentality – these too, these responses of the heart, must be held in abeyance. Only later when we come to reflect on the experience should we review it critically and examine our feelings. If in the first instance we do not absorb it fully, how can we reflect on it with understanding later? Submission, not conquest, is the way to enlightenment.

Criticism in this sense is a perfectly acceptable aftermath to the mystic experience. Comparison with literary accounts or with the experiences of personal friends can help us to check the validity of our own. And we need to be certain of the authenticity of our own vision if the memory of it, after the impact of the experience itself has faded over the years, is to remain freshly alive in the ever growing tree of our life.

* * *

In finding our way round a garden we also put our trust in it in a plainer, merely topographical sense. Its creator gives us guidance by way of paths, bridges, avenues, and flights of steps. But, acquiring its form over many years by frequent small adjustments to its creator's initial layout, and the growing to maturity of its trees and shrubs, the mystic garden comes to take on its present appearance as much from a multitude of chance events as from the completion of a preordained plan.

Paths that were once laid in a certain series of curves may alter their course over time as trampling feet broaden a curve here or elide one there and as plants grow over them from the side. Flowerbeds spread out imperceptibly as the rough edges are trimmed; ferns multiply and hide the rim of a pond; shrubs are pruned to allow room for other plants as well as for the garden's visitors. Nature and man interact; chance and design are unified. So the garden gradually approximates to an ideal form, an ideal that has reality but only in the gardener's imagination. Thus the way to its essential being is slowly perfected.

As the mystic garden matures over the years the continual exchange between man and nature means that it can never be symmetrical. But despite its asymmetry, *balance* may be a feature of the overall design in the placing of its trees, paths, statues, flowerbeds, lawns, hedges, but only as, for example, a small weight can balance a large one by being placed further away from the fulcrum, or as a tree can lean over almost to the point of toppling yet continue to support its crown by the weight of the trunk and strength of the roots. Though an approximation to symmetry is certainly common in nature as we see it in the form of many flowers or in leaf arrangements, or in the bilateral symmetry of many insects, it is never exact. We are apt to be disturbed by gross asymmetry in something that is by nature approximately symmetrical, especially if we are looking at a human body or face that departs much from its natural bilateral symmetry. But the exact symmetry we see in some crystals, for example, is not found in any living plant or animal.

Nor are two plants ever identical with each other. They may have the same sets of genes, but each plant has interacted with a different environment, and that will have established differences between the plants. No two things in nature are identical:

> *'"One blade of grass is like another blade of grass." In one sense, yes, but in a preciser sense, never.'*
>
> F. L. Lucas.[1]

So although at the anatomical level there is sometimes an approximation to symmetry, when we examine the whole plant in nature we find none. There are hardly perceptible differences between young plants with the same genetic constitution, but as they grow they are subjected to variations in the soil in which each is rooted, to differences in rainfall, exposure to sunlight, and the fall of snow that each experiences, and to differences in the pressures from neighbouring competitors, and all these differences are magnified in the mature plants to give irregularity of size, form, fertility, and life span, despite their genetic identity.

Identity, repetition, regularity, symmetry – nature abhors them all. But balance it relishes, though not indefinitely. A community of plants can maintain itself in balance for many years, though usually with annual fluctuations from various causes. But indefinitely, no. If it never changed, evolution would have ceased and time would have come to an end.

★ ★ ★

Paths not only mark the way in a garden. By their pattern and texture they adorn it. Whether they have a formal, architectural character or consist of little more than a loose arrangement of rocks as stepping stones (nearly all the most beautiful paths of either type are to be found in Japanese gardens), the relation to them of the plants alongside needs some thought.

Generally speaking, the smaller the garden the more incursive should shrubs and herbs be beside the path, even to the extent of impeding us as we walk along, for a small garden needs to be more intricate, more intimate, more obstructive, more slowly traversed than a large one. If we are slowed down by obtruding shrubs, we have time to examine the garden more minutely. And if in a sunny stretch the path is invaded by sweetly smelling marjoram, lavender, mint, and thyme and other aromatic plants, they will shed their perfume on the air as we brush against them. Contact with their leaves may make our legs a bit wet in rainy weather, but no garden lover can object to that.

★ ★ ★

In contrast to the (at least metaphorically) two-dimensional path stands the avenue, adding a third dimension with its skyward reach. Nothing like these creatures of co-operation between man and nature is found in the wild. Their straight or at least determinate lines (for they may follow the curve of a drive or, as in a yew avenue at Chatsworth, have a crinkle-crankle form), their regular course, the uniform spacing of the trees, and restriction to one or rarely two species present a far more symmetrical pattern than plants ever achieve in the wild.

It must be admitted they have sometimes been planted to serve a debased purpose, namely to inflate their owner's pride of possession, his standing in the countryside. As 'symbols of authority,' even as 'rows of soldiers standing to attention, or forming a guard of honour',[2] they serve at once to intimidate a visitor approaching between the towering trees the portals of the great house, and to flatter him through signalling the favour being conferred by his being admitted to such a splendid estate. Yet at their best, avenues are not out of place in a mystic garden, for they symbolise something that nature offers though never realises in that form, namely a beckoning vista to man.

Among the most striking avenues in the French geometrical style to be seen in an English garden are those at St Paul's Walden Bury (Hertfordshire), composed of clipped beech (formerly hornbeam). Radiating in straight lines through allées cut in deciduous woodland, the avenues (originally laid out in about 1730) have their severity mitigated by their being sited on undulating ground. Many of them offer the attractive vista of a temple or pavilion at the end, and one of them has incorporated the 'borrowed scenery' of a near-by church.

At Avebury Manor may be seen, on a much smaller scale, a yew avenue leading up to a statue. This favourite device of garden designers is complementary to the provision of a window in the hedge to concentrate attention on something specially attractive, but in contrast to the window the avenue invites us to walk straight along it, encourages us even to hurry along, to inspect the statue or whatever it may be at the far end – perhaps a garden seat on which we may rest.

Altogether on a different scale from these trim lines of clipped hedges are the avenues in which naturally grown trees soar above us to 60 or 100 feet (18–30 metres). An eye-stopper has been achieved by the use of monkey puzzles

'It is as though we were in one of the great cathedrals' (p. 85): Killerton's beech avenue.

(*Araucaria*) to form avenues at Bicton (Devon) and Castle Kennedy (Ayrshire). But for natural grandeur nothing surpasses beeches allowed to grow to their full height, as in the splendid avenue at Killerton (Devon). Here the horizontal vista through the lines of smooth grey trunks with the sun glancing across them is certainly part of the effect, but in addition we marvel at the way these pillars thrust up to the sky and bear aloft their canopy of branches, at their most beautiful on a sunny day in winter when they are leafless and filled with blue. It is as though we were in one of the great cathedrals, where our spirit leaps heavenward while the body stands dwarfed among the gothic pillars and we admire the intricate tracery in the roof far above.

As they gazed aloft among the criss-crossing arches the people in medieval times marvelled to see the stonework gradually being filled in, till the whole edifice almost seemed to hang in the air yet gave solidity in stone to man's prayers. Today when we follow in their footsteps and look up to the traceried roof, we wonder. For them certitude; for us a question.

★ ★ ★

Broad or narrow, crooked or straight, the lawn still provides the most popular highway in the gardens of the British Isles. Grass grows into a more velvety turf in these misty islands than in most other places. Paths and woodland rides, stepping stones and flights of steps, bridges and avenues all have their role in taking us from one part of a garden to another. But the lawn is still pre-eminent. On its yielding turf we can enjoy the pleasure of moving here or there on impulse. In its uniformity of colour and texture we enjoy a contrast to the drama of the flowers and shrubs in the neighbouring beds. It calms the mind and offers a basis of tranquillity from which to look at the rest of the garden. Like the face of an old friend, it is its familiarity that especially comforts us.

We may admire the daisies on a lawn or (speaking for myself) a mossy corner, but we do not examine it in detail. We take it for granted. The very ordinariness of a lawn whatever garden we are in means our response to it is habitual, uninquiring; we are so accustomed to its unobtrusive verdure that we hardly notice it. Like a habit, a lawn liberates the imagination.

Habit is a most creative force in the human mind, because it frees us for more important things. When we learn to drive a car, for instance, the control of its steering, gears, clutch, brakes, and so on occupies all our attention at first. But with practice and skill our management of the car becomes habitual, and we are free to concentrate on more important problems, notably the hazards of the road. Thus habit takes over from the anxious thought that kept us tense in the first place, and when it has done so we can turn our attention to something else. As we acquire more habits, so we extend the bounds of freedom.

In the same way the lawn settles the mind. It gives us a familiar background and does not engage our interest. We are free to inquire into the special character of the garden, to examine the beauty of its design and to feel the heart of nature beating within it. In seeking the way to the meaning of the garden we are glad to start from a good lawn for the foundation of freedom it gives us.

CHAPTER ELEVEN

Fulfilment

A garden is never complete. When a person who loves his garden stands contemplating it, he does not really see the garden around him. What he has in his mind is an ideal of the garden superimposed on the actuality and partly hiding it, but it is not an ideal of the kind he has to accept as unattainable. Rather, his vision is of an improved version of the present scene, of some planting here, some pruning there, and of some reshaping of lawn, path, or pergola. He is thinking of the next stage in an infinite series, not its final term at infinity. As an artist looks at the countryside before him and converts it into a landscape painting, so the gardener rearranges the scene in his mind's eye by moving some shrubs to a sunnier position and replacing some herbaceous plants with ones he hopes will thrive better.

But to speak of an ideal, with its connotation of a conclusion that can never be attained in practice, is appropriate here too, for when the gardener takes one step forward that he has in mind he knows that a further prospect will tempt him onwards – and on for ever. He is striving towards an ideal even while he remains doubtful what that ideal is or of the precise way his work will lead him. He can see so far along the perspective of his imagination, but the end, the fulfilment of that particular dream, is always beyond the horizon.

* * *

Both Christianity and Buddhism have grown over the centuries into complex faiths with elaborate rituals, and many sub-categories of both faith and ritual have become split off from the main stream of each. If their founders were to examine their progeny today, they might scarcely recognise the connection between these world religions and the teaching they themselves gave in their lifetime. So many saints and philosophers, so many holy men and ruling princes, hermits and potentates, preachers and mystics have added to the edifice by their zeal, or reason, or force of arms that whole libraries of exegesis and disputation have grown up round the original texts. Yet the living core remains. And without organic growth and evolution a religion, like a garden, becomes a death mask of something that once had joy, daring, vitality, mystery, revelation.

A great garden, like a great religion, starts with the ideas of one person, but it undergoes expansion and modification and reinterpretation. As it takes shape it matures in response not only to its owner's command but to philosophical ideas current in society at the time, literary and artistic tastes, and contemporary socio-horticultural fashion, the suggestions of his friends and the examples of his rivals. Then his heirs and successors take over, bringing new ideas and more, or less, money. Buildings are added or pulled down, trees and shrubs planted that had not been introduced to cultivation in Britain when the garden started life, and streams, ponds, fountains, and statues are enhanced or eroded with the passage of time. So through accretion and transformation a garden may come to represent not one only but a succession of changing cultures over the years. Places like Stowe and Stourhead are palimpsests that show us the history of human thought, in all its accidental development, as well as eternal secrets of human life.

If a garden ever reached completion in the sense that any alteration would impair it, the life would have gone out of it. The 'perfect' garden must lack something, for life itself is incomplete.

'What is most perfect seems to have something missing;
Yet its use is unimpaired.'

Tao Tê Ching, ch. 45.

★ ★ ★

Every gardener who enjoys his craft knows in his heart the fulfilment that comes from exercising it. Digging itself may be tiring work, but the more that is put into it the greater the satisfaction on looking back at the accomplished task (just as to run the most dangerous risks yields in retrospect the greatest sense of triumph). We feel drawn into a special understanding of nature as we prepare the ground in winter or plan improvements to the scene in summer, and a wave of hope buoys us up when we sow seeds in spring and plant bulbs in the autumn. To prune shrubs, stake flower spikes, tie in a wisteria, even to hoe out or pull up the weeds gives us the satisfaction that we are encouraging nature to do its best for us. Working in the garden teaches us, as no printed text can, the nature of the life that passes through our hands, and from that we learn something about the meaning of our own lives.

Yet even this cultivation of nature, so uniquely refreshing because we are not passive spectators but active participants, can be sadly abused. For just as pride of ownership has led the occasional landowner to regard his ha-ha as simply a device for impressing his visitors with the vast extent of his estate, and led another landowner to plant a great avenue with little thought but to dignify his house and overawe the carriage folk who approach it, so the harmless pursuit of horticulture can be made to serve a like pride in surpassing the meagre efforts of friends and rivals.

Everyone enjoys a colourful front garden or a well grown row of sweet peas without feeling the need to accuse their owner of vain display, but degeneration is apt to set in when the competition bench looms ahead. The growing of those delicious vegetables, leeks and marrows, simply to produce the greatest girth and weight at the expense of edibility is as grotesque as the care the King of Karague (now in Uganda) took in the nineteenth century over fattening his wives so prodigiously that they could not stand.

There have always been times when the imaginative interpretation of nature gave way to the mere cultivation of plants, but this waste of spirit has become prominent in Britain in the twentieth century. As well as innumerable species newly introduced with the aid of air travel we have seen an influx of hybrids and varieties as a result of the plant breeder's art. The beauty of a wild flower is a beauty without vanity. Yet man has almost succeeded in endowing some hybrids with this human failing, so that if they could find a voice they would murmur, 'Look at me!'

Surely one of the most dispiriting experiences must be to visit a national show of, say, daffodils and see how the demure flower we know in the river valleys of western Britain has been bred into a gross caricature of its wild self; or to visit an orchid show and see the contrast between the species that have evolved over millions of years and the hybrids bred in a few generations by man – flowers fit only for a plutocrat's buttonhole or bodice. We see hybrid lilies wholly lacking the refinement of flower that is such a distinctive mark of their race; roses whose flowers are a garish mixture of red and yellow, or with petals which, as they fade, clash in colour with those that are fresh; or herbaceous plants whose flowering stems are incapable of supporting themselves. Nor is this new; several centuries ago man turned his hand to converting wild primroses into the varieties with blowsy double flowers which flop to the ground from overweight, especially when wet. No wonder a high degree of skill in horticulture is needed to cope with these aberrations. And this, combined with a repugnance to any realistic contact with nature by a materialist society, has resulted in the loss of all deeper meaning from most contemporary gardens.

Vaguely aware of this loss but puzzled by how to remedy it, some gardeners have simply turned to the past and created 'period gardens,' sometimes, if they can afford them, with embellishment by antique statues and urns (often modern fakes, incidentally). They are wholly inappropriate to the twentieth century because they are meaningless to people who know virtually nothing of the classical world which gave them birth. Instead of the face of nature they show us a mask.

*   *   *

If a gardener looks for fulfilment through the symbol of natural life that the garden presents to him, he can do no less than ensure that each plant so far as possible attains fulfilment in its own terms. This does not mean that everything should run wild. A garden is not a wild place.

Nor does a plant necessarily find its natural fulfilment when it grows in isolation so that all its parts are fully developed. The placing of plants on their own came to be favoured by some practitioners of the 'gardenesque' style, and in defining what he meant by this term J. C. Loudon,[1] writing in 1838, used an ambiguous phrase: 'By the gardenesque style is to be understood the production of that kind of scenery which is best calculated to display the individual beauty of trees, shrubs and plants in a state of nature . . .' But in a state of nature plants rarely show their beauty in a form that could aptly be described as 'individual'. They are gregarious creatures. In a temperate climate such as ours, with an average rainfall varying from about 22 inches (560mm) in the east to over 100 inches (2500mm) in the west, plants are more often seen in their natural state as members of communities than as individuals, except in exposed places on mountains and moorland. The contrast is seen to perfection in sub-deserts, where suitable niches in the habitat are few and most of the plants are solitary in a waste of sand or rock. But in the temperate zones plants cover the ground and jostle each other for space, forming clumps and stands and drifts and carpets.

Consequently, if a garden is to present a symbol of its life in a naturalistic rather than, say, a geometric manner, it needs at least to suggest what is a particularly notable feature of wild vegetation. In their fertility and thrust for space it should show plants pressing upon each other, intermingling their branches, creeping over the edges of paths and walls, supporting and shading each other where appropriate, spreading their progeny to bare patches where this can be allowed without detriment to the overall design, and living healthy lives without chemical treatment. It is the fulfilment of natural life. That is what we put into it and what we draw out of it.

Just as the creation of a garden is a continuous process going on through the years, so the enjoyment of it grows with time. The original idea grows with the thought given to it by its owners and his friends and develops into a more elaborate realisation of his first vision; it becomes a part of the culture of the day. In contemplation of it we enlarge our vision with the perspective of other cultures while at the same time drawing on the eternal source of our existence in nature.

CHAPTER TWELVE

Harmony

The Herdmen

What pleasure have great princes,
More dainty to their choice,
Than herdmen wild, who careless
In quiet life rejoice,
And Fortune's fate not fearing
Sing sweet in summer morning?

Anon.[1]

THE delights of the simple life close to nature have been celebrated at least from the civilisation of classical Greece onwards. It is true that the delight has generally been the more intense as the distance from rural toil increased, yet chained though they were to gaining a living from the soil many peasants, herdmen, and hunters acquired a dignified patience with their lot that townsmen and courtiers have often noted to be lacking in themselves. Or at least in their friends. Life close to 'nature' has always held a lure for sophisticated people as the embodiment of simplicity, kindliness, endurance, and equanimity.

But in the Renaissance a very different attitude to nature became prominent. For in contrast to nature the Mother, all forgiving, ever nourishing, who always received back her troubled sons and daughters with love, people began to think of nature as something that could be readily exploited, just because it ministered to man's needs so effectually. More than that: control over nature became the hallmark of civilisation in the western world.

The Renaissance garden (of which no authentic example remains in Britain) was, according to Sir Roy Strong,[2] the province of the architect – where man completely controlled his environment. Moreover:

'It was a symbol of pride and an expression of royal and aristocratic magnificence; man conquered the earth, tilled and planted it, subjecting it to his will.'

The simplicity of medieval gardens was overborne by the showy splendour of the Renaissance. Intricate patterns reminiscent of the robes worn at court rather than of the flowery meadows where lovers walked in spring were laid out on rectangular parterres so as to be admired from the upper windows of the house. As in the French geometric gardens of the seventeenth century, which grew out of the Italian sixteenth century gardens, plants had in themselves no individuality. They were no more than colourful ciphers, and their life was subsumed into filling the role, as it were, of a knot in a tapestry, a stitch in some embroidery.

Among the earliest rebels against this weaving of nature in the designs of pattern books were Francis Bacon (1561–1626) and Henry Wotton (1568–1639). Both accepted in the main that gardens should be of formal design, and Bacon, a forerunner of the experimental scientists who came to prominence later in the century, held like them to the belief in man's complete dominion over nature. Yet in a well known passage he inveighed against the artificiality of the patterned flower-beds of his day:

> *'As for the Making of* Knots, *or* Figures, *with* Divers Coloured Earths, *that they may lie under the Windowes of the House, on that Side, which the* Garden *stands, they be but Toyes: You may see as good sights, many times, in Tarts.*[3]

Wotton, poet and ambassador, and author of the description of an ambassador as 'an honest man sent abroad to lie for the good of his country,' went further than Bacon in advocating a degree of informality in gardens that to us seems to look forward a century or so:

> *'First, I must note a certaine contrairietie between* building *and* gardening: *For as Fabriques should bee* regular, *so Gardens should bee* irregular, *or at least cast into a very wilde* Regularitie.'[4]

As the seventeenth century advanced and the first glimmers of experimental science appeared, the formation of the Royal Society coincided with a split that developed in attitudes to nature. While the 'philosophers' (whom we should now call scientists) turned to the treatment of nature with the object of establishing man's complete control over it for his own benefit, the poets wrote of it as a gentle, innocent domain where man might find solace from the cares of state after the day's work:

'When nibbling sheep at large pursue their food,
And unmolested kine rechew the cud;
When curlews cry beneath the village walls,
And to her straggling brood the partridge calls . . . .'
Anne Finch, Countess of Winchilsea, *A Nocturnal Reverie.*

And that epitome of nature, the garden, came to be seen as a place not where man imposed his will on untamed creation, transforming rudeness into civilisation, but rather where he could enjoy the bounty given by Providence.

The Garden of Eden in Milton's account of it, where regular lines and ordered plantings might have been expected to symbolise the dominion of its Creator, did not resemble any contemporary garden with which he might have been familiar but, rather, heralded one of the landscape gardens that came into existence in the next century:

'A happy rural seat of various view;
Groves whose rich Trees wept odorous Gumms and Balme . . .
Betwixt them Lawns, or level Downs, and Flocks
Grasing the tender herb, were interpos'd,
Of palmie hilloc, or the flourie lap
Of som irriguous Valley spread her store,
Flours of all hue, and without Thorn the Rose:
Another side, umbrageous Grots and Caves . . .'
Paradise Lost, Book 4.

Milton's younger contemporary Marvell also lamented the tricks that 'Luxurious Man' enforced on the garden and preferred the wild and innocent face of nature:

'Tis all enforced; the Fountain and the Grot,
While the sweet fields do lie forgot:
Where willing nature does to all dispence
A wild and fragrant innocence.'

The Mower against Gardens.

These visions of nature which began to influence thought in the seventeenth century gained strength and clarity in the eighteenth. The English garden threw off the formality of French and Dutch design; the geometry of their canals and parterres joined the earlier 'Tarts' and 'Fabriques' on the rubbish heap, and such writers as Addison, Pope, and Horace Walpole now gave expression to the burgeoning English philosophy of nature as a benign world with a life of its own in harmony with that of man. Man's inner life became one with life beyond the ha-ha. Just as Cézanne defined painting as a harmony parallel with nature,[5] so eighteenth century landowners and landscape gardeners saw their parks as representing a like harmony.

* * *

Nature's harmony, enjoyed by Adam and Eve in Milton's Garden of Eden with 'simplicities and spotless innocence,' was equally enjoyed by the animals there:

'About them frisking playd
All Beasts of th'Earth, since wilde, and of all chase
In Wood or Wilderness, Forrest or Den;
Sporting the Lion ramped, and in his paw
Dandl'd the Kid; Bears, Tygers, Ounces, Pards,

Gambold before them, th'unwieldy Elephant
To make them mirth us'd all his might, and wreathd
His Lithe Proboscis . . . .'

Paradise Lost, Book 4

Milton's words 'since wilde' indicate clearly enough that he understood the untamable character most animals had acquired since Eden faded from the map and men had begun to cast a mathematical eye upwards at the heavens. We today are even more conscious of the unceasing struggle of living organisms, whether plants or animals, to occupy space in which to mature and from which to disseminate their progeny. Shrubs and trees over thousands of square miles compete for life with the unwieldy elephant, and if a lion gets a kid in his paw he eats it.

Yet the dream remains. Though we know the creatures of nature are a mêlée of predators and prey, there are many fine gardens we have only to visit to feel a sense of peace descend upon us. The tranquillity of a rounded hill clothed with trees and shrubs, the placidity of a lake bringing the glittering light of the sky down into the park, a tree-lined path which gives a succession of glimpses over the water, the shelter of an old oak's spreading branches, the gentle green of mosses on a bank – all express a nature at peace and, as we walk in the open landscape or the woodland, a peace that enters us and leaves its impress on our unquiet lives. It makes no difference what time of year we visit the sort of gardens that have these powers. Any garden can look delightful in spring and summer, just as a youthful face readily lights up with joy. But what when winter comes? Then it is the intensity of life its owner has experienced that moves us, as in an old face, and the intensity of his genius that has tempered the garden.

It is man's vision of the Garden of Eden, not the real world of nature, that imbues these gardens with their special character, and visitors to them today enjoy a re-creation of that vision. Man's spirit comes into accord with the spirit of the landscape as he wanders through it. Here indeed we 'sing sweet in summer morning.' Art has taken over from nature, for the function of art is to bring us into harmony with the world around us, to make it tolerable to lives that are often in discord with their destiny. There was no art in the Garden of Eden. Art is a consequence of the Fall.

⋆ ⋆ ⋆

There is another lesson too we can learn from nature, and likewise from nature's messenger, the garden. Nature is indifferent to man's ideas of right and wrong and unmoved by the ethical aspirations that variously influence us. Conduct that in man we may judge aggressive, or selfish, or pacific, or cunning, or cruel has no such meaning in nature. People who can accept that nature stands outside man's judgement are satisfied, indeed enthralled, to observe wildlife for what it is, on its own terms. This in itself brings the gift of sympathetic understanding. Man is one thing, wild nature another. For us to learn the secrets of nature as they really are, and not as we are inclined to judge them by human criteria, sets our own lives into a universal perspective.

All living organisms are the products of evolution. We all share the same pool of genes; in one mixture they produce a spider, in another a seaweed, in another a man. The harmony of a mystic garden lies in its blending of Heaven and Earth.* The recognition in our hearts that in a biological sense, or in the eyes of God, we are all members of the living creation brings order, peace, and love into our lives.

Now in the twentieth century we have become conscious of the enormous perils we risk in dominating the natural world with our advanced technology. The fact is, man is unfit for mastery.

* cf. Suzuki:[6] 'The principle of *cha-no-yu* [the art of the tea ceremony in Japan] is the spirit of the harmonious blending of Heaven and Earth and provides the means for establishing universal peace.'

CHAPTER THIRTEEN

Awakening

IT is a warm summer's afternoon in the garden. A comfortable chair is set in the dappled shade of a tree. I snooze away, sunk in sleep, dreamless, relaxed, inert. Then, as consciousness slowly returns, fragmentary visions drift across the mind. Mostly they embody in barely recognisable form the preoccupations of the previous few days, but gradually, just as the sun dissolves the mist over water, they swirl up into wraiths, disperse, and reveal a clearer scene. Impressions from the garden itself take over; the outlines of reality begin to return through every drowsy sense. A robinia 'Frisia' is lit up yellow in the sunlight; some begonias brighten a corner with a patchwork of pink, yellow, red, and white, and in the shade a group of hartstongue ferns spear the air with their fronds. To the visual beauty of the garden is added the music of buzzing insects providing a bass ground to the cooing of a distant wood pigeon, and the sent of a buddleia drifts over like aerial honey. As the afternoon sun seeps through my own skin I taste the sun-warmed flesh of a plum, and then I go on to enjoy the texture of various leaves by running my fingers over them – hairy, glossy, papillose, ribbed, leathery, silky, or hispid. The pleasures of the garden flood in through every sense – sight, hearing, smell, temperature, taste, touch – pleasures as varied as any work of art can offer. So it is not surprising that the garden has seemed to be a dangerously sinful place to those stern philosophers who considered that the enjoyment of the world obtained through our senses is distracting and debasing, while that obtained through the contemplation of ideas is uplifting.

In medieval times the Christian Platonists, notably St Anselm (1033–1109), who was Archbishop of Canterbury in 1093–1109, were specifically aware of the moral risks posed by gardens owing to the variety of senses that they stimulated. Today those dangers would be generally regarded as exaggerated, yet there is a lesson for us here. Where I would venture to differ from St Anselm is in his *opposing* the sensory to the symbolic. For the pleasures that gardens give us through our senses should be regarded, I believe, as an invitation, an exciting transition, to the enlightenment we seek through contemplation of its secrets, not as a distraction from the accomplishment of that quest.*

Then the first phase of awaking is overidden as our intellect disperses the sensory pleasures and we begin to examine the source of the scents that fill the air, or to consider why some plants have smooth leaves, others bristly; to study which particular species and cultivars go well together, why some plants have thrived and some failed, and which would be better for a move elsewhere. Thought has taken over from sensation. Equally enjoyable in a different way is the

* I agree with the thought that Hester Thrale, friend and confidante of Samuel Johnson, jotted down in her notebook: 'I have often observ'd, Business disqualifies a man for heaven more than Pleasure does.'[1]

intellectual pleasure we derive from studying the problems of this garden and those of other gardens we have visited.

Sharp, clear observation of the scene occupies us, and we begin to think about its special features, to compare it, criticise it, admire it. Yet still the heart of it eludes our deepest understanding. Intensity of sensation, depth of feeling, acuity of intellect – all are necessary for true enlightenment, but they are only introductory: in themselves they are not enough. I believe St Anselm would agree with that.

Mere pleasure pouring in through the senses, though not in the least to be despised, lacks co-ordination until we begin to reflect upon it. Very young children cannot extract its meaning, since their world is a more directly sensory experience than ours, and it does adults a power of good to revert at times to purely sensory reception, to experience the thing simply as a source of impressions, unclassified and unnamed, a naked experience without the barrier of thought and its consequent interpretation of meaning.

But conversely the intellect can yield some of the keenest pleasures we know. What scientist has not felt a literally physical excitement, his whole being alive and tingling, as he makes a series of observations or experiments that gradually at first, and then in a flash, bring certitude to what was previously only guessed at, draw into the realm of knowledge what until then had lain buried in ignorance? To realise that one has crossed the threshold from the known into the unknown and made a valid discovery is among the most exhilarating experiences life has to offer. Perhaps an artist working now furiously, now laboriously, to establish the uniqueness of his vision, and to transfer that vision to canvas, is overwhelmed by that same joy of creation which lies at the heart of all life.

It is no wonder that, for people who love nature with the single-minded devotion of a landscape painter or a naturalist, the dedication of their lives to nature's reign comes near to a religion. The artist who more than any other in the last hundred years or so taught us to see nature with a fresh eye, Monet, began to go blind in old age and felt he could do no more at times. Kenneth Clark[2] records how the painter's friend, Georges Clemenceau the statesman, would then drive down to his studio and beg him to take up his brush.

> *'Once more Monet would immerse himself,'* Lord Clark tells us, *'in his pool of memories and sensations. Total immersion: this is the ultimate reason why the love of nature has been for so long accepted as a religion. It is a means by which we can lose our identity in the whole and gain thereby a more intense consciousness of being.'*

★ ★ ★

To halt at the sensory enjoyment of a garden, or at the intellectual appreciation of its treasures, is to leave our quest uncompleted. Beautiful the garden may be, a picture at which we gaze enraptured by the sheer profusion of its flowers, the balance and clash and harmony of colour; and its plants may arouse botanical or horticultural discussion on whether they can withstand polluted air, a winter temperature of 10°C, and so on. But aesthetic and scientific appreciation are no more than the twin pillars of the gate through which we must pass to reach a deeper understanding of the garden's life. For beyond the appearances, beyond the trees and flowers and ornaments, beyond the blue sky in the lake and the green shelter of the woodland, lies the secret of our kinship with nature, in which the self fades away and we attain a new intensity of living.

CHAPTER FOURTEEN

Serenity

FROM earliest civilisation the notion of infinity has puzzled man. What is it? And where? What distinguishes it? Are *infinite* wisdom, goodness, and mercy attributes of God?

'Infinity has a tendency to fill the mind with that sort of delightful horror, which is the most genuine effect, and truest test of the sublime.'

Edmund Burke, *A Philosophical Enquiry into the Origin of our Ideas of the Sublime and Beautiful.*

Even young children are fascinated by infinity. No sooner do they grasp the concept of enumeration than they amuse themselves and irritate their elders by counting up to large and ever larger numbers – thousands, millions, billions, and more. 'What is the biggest number you can imagine?' they ask. Or, as my three-year-old grandson was heard to say in the midst of his calculations, 'How big is God's bottom?' At that age they know what Blake meant by:

'To see a World in a Grain of Sand
And a Heaven in a Wild Flower,

'That age-old universal symbol, a circle set in a square' (p. 110): Knightshayes.

Hold Infinity in the palm of your hand
And Eternity in an hour.'

Auguries of Innocence.

Later on as school children they begin to puzzle over the vastness of the universe, the physical turmoil of its galaxies and the death of matter as it falls into black holes. 'Is space infinite?' they wonder and 'Is time?' And when they grow up to become lovers they promise each other an infinitude of kisses, of understanding, of kindness, of happiness, though later some ask sadly as infinity no longer beckons and they sink in on themselves:

'Why,then, latterly did we not speak,
Did we not think of those days long dead,
And ere your vanishing strive to seek
That time's renewal? We might have said,
"In this bright spring weather
We'll visit together
Those places that once we visited."'

Thomas Hardy, *The Going.*

* * *

Nowhere is the paradox of infinity brought home to us more beautifully than at Knightshayes (Devon). Between the house and the woodland garden is a square enclosure with high walls of clipped yew.* The floor consists of a lawn about 28 yards

* It is just not square, but the difference between length and breadth is inappreciable to the naked eye.

(25 metres) across in which is set a circular pond 13 yards (12 metres) in diameter. Near the north-west margin of the pond a carefully pruned weeping pear (*Pyrus salicifolia*) hangs its silver leaved branches near the water's edge, while from a niche in the northern wall of yew a charming statue overlooks the scene.

We have here that age-old universal symbol, a circle set in a square. (It is a favourite pattern too for water basins in Japanese temple gardens.) At Knightshayes the glittering circle of water and the square of yew hedges enclosing it compose a perfect work of art that can be admired irrespective of the season. The weeping tree at the water's edge and the statue in its niche mitigate what might otherwise be a forbidding severity in the composition, and the plane surface of the pond is itself ruffled here and there by a few water lilies. Yet this unassuming scene introduces us to the mystery that puzzled men from early Greek times onwards, namely the relation between the finite and the infinite. They saw the problem geometrically as how to 'square the circle,' that is, how to construct a circle of the same area as a given square. We now know that the problem is insoluble in rational terms; we cannot close the gap between the finite and the infinite. But the marriage of circle and square through art succeeds in creating aesthetic harmony out of rational dissonance. In the resolution of this paradox the temporal is unified with the eternal, and the serene circle of water lying in its enclosure imparts to us a hint of our finite creation at the hands of an infinite creator.

★ ★ ★

Serenity is attained only after we have travelled a long journey. It is not another name for the passive enjoyment we receive in a garden when it lulls our senses with its charms; still less has serenity any resemblance to the self-satisfaction we may feel on looking at our own garden and thinking it good. Rather, we set a course in the right direction when we learn to examine an unfamiliar idea with sympathy. To accept rather than to judge takes us along the way, for acceptance is the foundation of wisdom. If we have not first accepted life, or death, we cannot hope to penetrate its meaning.

★ ★ ★

From earliest times water has been valued as an emblem of the serene acceptance of the natural way of things.

> *'The highest good is like that of water. The goodness of water is that it benefits the ten thousand creatures; yet itself does not scramble, but is content with the places that all men disdain. It is this that makes water so near to the Way.'*
>
> *Tao Tê Ching*. ch. 8.

Wells and grottoes dedicated to water spirits were a common feature of Georgian gardens, and may be seen today for example at Rousham, Stourhead, and Sezincote among others. Certainly the owners of these estates, in making obeisance to beliefs that had long since died out in the circles in which they moved, were doing no more than reminding us of the erstwhile power that such spirits wielded in classical times, though among simpler people in the eighteenth century and on into the twentieth old animistic beliefs in the actual

'Destiny and chance are complementary attributes of the same jet of water' (p. 113): Bicton.

presence of spirits in pools and woods and rocky knolls lingered on, as I personally know from my boyhood in Devon.

Nor has the romance of the old ways quite vanished. Everyone has felt the magic of standing at the edge of a pool and peering into its dark depths; or gazing over the sky-filled, reed-margined surface of a lake winding away round a wooded promontory to disappear among the trees. And who has not enjoyed leaning over a bridge to watch a stream rippling through its arches? Perhaps the sprites have now vanished underground, but in our imagination we still delight to fill their old ledges and niches with watchful figures.*

The fascination of a fountain is that, though the droplets individually follow an unpredictable course, the pattern they compose in their trajectory hardly changes from one moment to another. Destiny and chance are complementary attributes of the same jet of water lit up as the sunlight falls on it and the droplets splash with a hypnotic whisper into the surrounding pool. So with a human life. Reflecting on its flow through time we switch back and forth in trying to interpret its course. At one instant we seem to stare backward over a long chain of cause and effect, at another we detect with bewilderment nothing but a succession of unrelated chances governing the same events.

In nature water does not struggle, though it may certainly flow with a mighty, an effortless force; so in a garden fountain it is better not wrenched and hurled this way and that, however effective such drama may be in city squares. Nor should

* The eye should always *look down* upon water, as Shenstone[1] emphasised. Hidcote has a circular pool in a tank with a stone wall about one metre high; because the water is at waist level, it presents a most disconcerting appearance.

a pool be allowed to depart from a natural simplicity and become cluttered with plants, lest it lose the particular qualities by means of which water imbues the imagination with serenity, namely its clarity, placidity, reflectiveness, transparency, and stability. Still water is best come upon in a secluded part of the garden, a secret garden, for contemplation; in an open and public place a fountain or gurgling mask is more appropriate.

Even a swiftly moving river has a constant face. Like a living organism, its substance is for ever changing while its form remains constant. The pattern of wavelets and eddies remains stable day after day; it falls through a weir of boulders, and then it feathers out white at their base, but its ridges and furrows retain their form year after year, and vary only slowly as the surface of the rocks becomes overgrown with cushions of mosses and liverworts. In a garden fortunate enough to have a stream flowing through it between grassy banks we can sit at the edge and watch the reflection of irises on its farther shore outlined against the sky in the surface of the water. In the mirrored image their leafy spears stand motionless against a clump of dark trees behind them, yet the surface reflecting them is in perpetual motion. The molecules of water never cease to flow, so that not for a second, not for an infinitesimal fraction of a second, is the water stationary, yet the portrait of trees and sky we see in it lies still as in a mirror. The water passes by: the image stays.

The natural world flows on through time unceasingly, but reflected from it to the eye of faith is a landscape whose lines express the assured serenity of a painting by Nicolas Poussin. Motion and stillness are united.

CHAPTER FIFTEEN

Illumination

AT the end of our contemplation of the mystic garden we hope to reach that depth of understanding, that horizon of freedom, we call illumination. But what *is* illumination? And where *are* the mystic gardens? The answers to these two questions lie deeper than they might seem to do at first sight, and to express them in words is like trying to describe Beethoven's fifth symphony to someone who has never heard it. The experience itself has something that no description can give.

Knowledge must surely be counted a useful preliminary to any human endeavour provided we are not deceived into thinking it is all we need and provided we jettison it later in the journey. Illumination lies much further ahead. A long journey through the mind, with emotional upheavals on the way, may have to be undertaken in the quest. Yet there is nothing inaccessible about it.

When Jesus went up into the mountain to preach to his disciples he told them:

> *'Ask, and it shall be given you; seek, and ye shall find; knock, and it shall be opened unto you . . .'*
>
> *St Matthew*, 7,7 (Authorised King James version).

He was speaking of illuminations as the word is used here. Life suddenly becomes infinitely worth living; its prospects excite us as old anxieties are smoothed away. Doubt gives way to assurance, hesitation to eagerness. We feel we can accomplish any task, however exhausting, undergo any trial, however heroic.

Consciousness expands beyond the limits of the self and we are filled with a sense of freedom, attainment, bliss. The boundaries of our life collapse like an old wall given a push, and we feel we are experiencing reality directly, a reality undistorted by preconceptions and unclouded by our accumulated memories. The hills are greener, the gorse smells sweeter, and we are attuned in harmony with nature, not the nature of myth and legend but the beating heart of our universe, where the plants and animals whose genes we share are ever striving to achieve their own fulfilment.

Though illumination is certainly not the same as being in love, the sense of liberation at the loss of self in something overwhelmingly greater, which they both share, makes the comparison possible. It is a state to which most of the great religions attach supreme value. Christianity, Judaism, Islam, Buddhism (especially Zen), and Taoism (which is hardly a religion) all have room for mystics in the varieties of experience they offer to seekers after the ultimate truth as distinct from the partial truth which is all that the use of reason alone can lead us to, and all prescribe rituals and disciplines to help the inquirer on his way. The illumination their mystics have recorded as themselves experiencing has varied in its symbolic content from one religion to another, but the state of unity with the Creator of all things that they have described is recognisably the same whatever the faith that inspired it.

Outside the religious disciplines there are other ways to illumination, and the mystic garden offers one of them. If contemplated with an act of faith so that we enter into its symbolic presentation of nature, the garden can help us to leave behind our daily selves and enter into its kingdom, that is, God's kingdom.

★ ★ ★

Many gardens have a quality that suddenly takes us by surprise and holds our attention. It may be only in a small part – a pool, the twist of a path, a woodland view, a stream running through a clump of trees – or the whole landscape may strike us as being a symbol of man and nature perfected.

Nowhere is a sense of union with nature more intimately felt than in some of the fine woodland gardens established from Sussex westwards along southern England, and then up through west Wales to the western coasts and islands of Scotland. What makes our contact with nature especially close in these gardens is that the vegetation enfolds us all round. Their mossy paths and banks cushion our way among the shrubs, and these brush our shoulders as we walk past them in a winding course that presents a succession of views through the woodland of a lake or a stream tumbling through a ravine or, at the coast, the sea hissing at us on the rocks far below. Above us the trees form a canopy of branches through which patches of sky and sunlight glitter or the rain comes pattering down.

But sadly the idyll often falls short of perfection. Many of the great woodland gardens are creations in the nineteenth and twentieth centuries of owners whose chief desire was to grow as many as possible of the new species of rhododendrons (and subsequently their hybrids) that were introduced, first from the New World, and then from the Himalayan foothills and the mountain ranges of Burma and China. These shrubs together with camellias and magnolias, davidias and tulip trees, dogwoods and hoherias set the gardens alight in the flowering season, which may amount to four months of the year, with a few stragglers outside those limits. But when not in flower many of the shrubs are a visual burden in a landscape that has no design. Whatever the season one of Kent's or Brown's or Repton's landscapes remains deeply satisfying as a portrayal of nature at its most sympathetic to man. But too many woodland gardens, once the camellias and magnolias and rhododendrons have ceased to enchant us with their flowers, have no structure to hold our attention, no character in their face; the foliage repels us with its monotony. For it is unfortunate that many of the evergreen shrubs which will tolerate our climate have dingy leaves – whose underside incidentally is often more attractive then the upper.

In a few of these gardens autumn tints again bring the place to life, with the brilliant reds, yellows, and oranges of maples, nyssa, fothergilla, liquidamber, and even the humble birch. Particularly notable in this respect is the High Beeches (West Sussex), one of the most charming of small woodland gardens owing to its setting in a combe, filled with bluebells in spring; in the autumn the myriad flaming shrubs on the hillside are a match for any sunset. Lovely in a different way is the garden at Leonardslee (West Sussex) with its lakes surrounded by groves of trees on the sloping sides of a valley. And Exbury garden (Hampshire) presents a woodland floor lit up by pools and bubbling streams, beside which the paths lead us on a walk through an idealised picture of nature.

The coastal gardens further west in the British Isles, though glorious when the shrubs are in flower, become less attractive during the rest of the year owing to their lack of good landscaping. But an inland garden, Minterne (Dorset), deserves emphasis for its beautiful layout in a valley and its lush growth of flowering shrubs and trees, primulas, ferns, and even the attractive (if invasive) giant horsetail (*Equisetum telmateia*).

Finally and among the most beautiful of all are two gardens loved by thousands in south-east England (and from much further afield) which, though not wholly woodland gardens, are predominantly so, namely Sheffield Park (East Sussex) and the Savill gardens in Windsor Great Park (Berkshire). Both are dream landscapes of wood and lake, stream and grove, and flowering shrubs and herbs, as lively with colour in autumn as in spring; and owing to their skilful disposition of bridges over the lakes and streams we can lean over the parapets and observe from many viewpoints the reflections of the trees shimmering in the water and setting it alight in autumn.

Judged by the reality of nature, all these woodland gardens are strikingly artificial, much more so than Lancelot Brown's landscapes, for instance. Yet with mysterious power the best of them evoke the kind of scene which Samuel Palmer delineated with brooding intensity in his youth. Some, too, in the exuberance of their vegetation, with their rhododendrons bearing shiny leaves as though cut from metal, their swaying

'Lush growth of flowering shrubs and trees, primulas, ferns' (p. 119): Minterne.

ferns and palms, their camellia flowers with all the regularity of a kaleidoscope pattern, and their shrubs at once dense, statuesque, and exotic, even call to mind a jungle such as the Douanier Rousseau might have painted. But, however remote from actuality, so compellingly, so overwhelmingly, with their riotous foliage do the best of these gardens embrace us that we are easily persuaded to believe they have the power deep down to open our eyes to their private realm. As we watch and listen, we hear the breath of nature stirring through the trees.

* * *

A journey through the mystic garden is a search for meaning beyond ourselves. For most people in the materialist culture that we have created, life holds little more than pushing a trolley along a supermarket floor, taking a wife, a husband, children, food, and household goods down from the shelves and paying for them at the checkout. Is there life beyond the checkout?

My belief is that many people hope there is but cannot actually experience it. Their soul, like the soul of their gardens, is buried beyond sight and sound and feeling, just as nature, whether real or ideal, lies forgotten among the container plants they have brought back from the garden centre and planted higgledy-piggledy. Then the proud owner waits for a few weeks' growth before inviting his neighbours in to admire the scene.

In contrast the mystic garden offers to its friends a pathway to another world. But if we are looking for a gazetteer of mystic gardens, then we have to admit that no such guide can be compiled. It is true that many of the gardens mentioned here have qualities which, when sought out with an aim to their deeper understanding, lead us on to that attunement with nature we seek in the journey towards illumination. They hold our eye, and we hear the soft command, 'Seek, and ye shall find.' And as we enter them we need to remember that, just as beauty is in the eye of the beholder, so understanding is in the eye of the faithful.

The name 'mystic garden' does not denote any garden of which one can say that its particular design holds the secret of the direct experience of nature as God's handiwork, or of nature as the cradle of man and the context of his freedom. Rather, a mystic garden shows us the way, or one of the infinite number of ways, by which we can attain a deeper knowledge of our existence. But though some gardens with a more adventurous spirit than others challenge our hesitancy, and point the way into the interior, the mystic garden itself has no place on the map: it lies in the soul of each of us.

Appendices

Appendices

Appendix 1
Emblematic Plants (p. 21)

The symbolism with which gardens as a whole were imbued from the early Middle Ages up to the nineteenth century is not to be confused with the emblematic associations that have long been attached to individual plants and flowers. Many works of art, whether paintings, stained glass in churches, or illuminated manuscripts, have made us familiar with the significance of plants in the vast realm of sacred mythology. The madonna lily has been the emblem of the Virgin Mary since early in the Christian era; the vine too was an early symbol of Christ from his words, 'I am the true vine' (*St John*, 15, 1); the white columbine, owing to its resemblance to a dove, symbolises the Holy Ghost, and clover has a clear association with the Trinity. Many abstract qualities too were personified in flowers. The lowly violet, for instance, symbolised humility, the evergreen ivy immortality, the simple daisy the innocence of the Christ child, and so on.[1]

The emblematic nature of many plants evolved in the imagination of mankind in prehistoric times. For example, the ancient Britons ('Druids') worshipped the oak and the spirit of the woodland grove that it embodied, and they likewise held the mistletoe (which so rarely grows on oak) in reverent awe. In Roman mythology the myrtle was a symbol of love. Thereafter it had a curious history. In medieval times, by an imaginative correlation of the Old Testament with the life of Christ, it came to represent the gentiles whom Christ converted: 'In the night I had a vision in which I saw a man among the myrtles in a hollow; he was on a bay horse and behind him were other horses, bay, sorrel, and white. "What are these, sir?" I asked, and the angel who was talking with me answered, "I shall show you what they are." Then the man standing among the myrtles said, "They are those whom the Lord has sent to range throughout the world."' (*Zechariah*, 1, 8–9).

The rose has had a particularly varied history as symbol. Making its earliest literary appearance as a European flower in Hellenic poetry, it became association with the deities of love in both Greek and Roman mythology. So by medieval times it was an established emblem that could be readily transferred to Christ, the God of Love. Thence the white rose, an emblem of purity, became associated with the Virgin Mary, while the red rose symbolised the blood of her martyred Son.[2]

Today, though these symbols have lost the power that once made them live, the 'language of flowers' still finds a place in greetings sent to friends, and folk memories of old beliefs prompt the bride to carry to her wedding a bouquet composed of appropriate flowers in season (some with pre-christian connotations) – perhaps orange blossom for purity, roses or myrtle for love, rosemary as a gift for the bridegroom and a symbol of remembrance.

Appendix 2
Crime Diminished (p. 21)

(p. 21)

An objective study of planning and architectural theory that has governed the building of many estates in twentieth century Britain has shown that in practice, so far from creating attractive, or even acceptable, places in which to live, it has in many ways actually been conducive to the rise of violence and vandalism on them. Professor Alice Coleman, of King's College, London, reported some results of her research to the British Association for the Advancement of Science at its annual meeting in 1991. Among them was the finding that the most powerful [beneficial] effect on the volume of crime was the presence of a semi-private space in the form of individual front and back gardens under the direct control of each ground-floor household. New front gardens in one estate were said to have transformed the menacing, anonymous gangs into polite individuals, and on another estate even racial harassment was reported to have been 'killed stone dead'. (I am indebted to Professor Coleman for a copy of her address.)

Lord Kames, the eighteenth century Scottish judge, presented[1] much the same view of social violence in his own day:

'Rough uncultivated ground, dismal to the eye, inspires peevishness and discontent: may not this be one cause of the harsh manners of savages? . . . Other fine arts may be perverted to excite irregular, and even vicious emotions: but gardening, which inspires the purest and most refined pleasures, cannot fail to promote every good affection.'

Appendix 3
Plant Forms (p. 35)

The form that a plant assumes as it matures provides one means of obtaining contrast in a garden, and it may be striking enough in itself to evoke in us an imaginative response. For instance, a well-placed, lone fastigiate tree pointing like a pillar to the sky puts us on the alert, asserts its life as a leader among the plants around it, as it attracts the eye, holds our attention, and draws our steps towards its commanding stance. In contrast, a weeping tree, a willow or ash perhaps, softens the horizon and induces a sense of ease, of relaxation. We enjoy the comfort of its branches as they glide downhill. Though of no less assured a form than the fastigiate tree, it brings a calm, rounded life to suggest that, despite the endless struggle in the natural world, there are moments when it is at peace.

Between these two life forms are those trees and shrubs with horizontally spreading branches. All too few can withstand our cool temperate climate (they are much more numerous in the tropics). Pre-eminent among them is the cedar of Lebanon, with its dark branches held out like the arms of a colossus cast in bronze. On a smaller scale we have *Cornus controversa*, which grows from a shrub into a tree after some years, and its equally horizontally branched relative, the shrubby *Cornus alternifolia.* (Unfortunately these are too often seen in their variegated forms. When lighting up a shady grove the pale-mottled leaves are attractive – at a distance. But the drawback to variegation in many plants, and notably in these *Cornus* species, is that when the leaves are examined individually they are seen to be distorted and even to seem diseased. This is due to a difference in growth rates between the green parts that contain a normal amount of chlorophyll and the pale parts that contain very little.) Another shrub with horizontal branching and, in addition, attractive flowers, is *Viburnum plicatum (tomentosum)*, especially the cultivar 'Mariesii.' In a less distinctive manner several of the large cotoneasters assume a broadly spreading habit in maturity, as in their delicate way do some of the Japanese maples. Yet, all told, few indeed of our trees and shrubs have what has always seemed to me this most attractive form of growth. Stability, serenity, guardianship, confidence, even compassion – these are the qualities they seem to impart to us as they stretch out over the turmoil of life in the garden.

Appendix 4
Mazes and Labyrinths (p. 59)

One of the most potent and complex symbols to have sprung from the myth-making recesses of man's unconscious mind is the maze, or labyrinth. (These terms, respectively from northern Europe [?Old English] and southern Europe [Greek], if not quite interchangeable idiomatically, are not distinguishable in their meaning.) In recent years many new ones have been constructed in public and private gardens both in Great Britain and overseas.

The origins of the labyrinth in antiquity are unknown, but they lie at least as far back as 2000 BC in Egypt.[1] The later Cretan labyrinth is known from legends given literary form in the fifth and fourth centuries BC but current orally some centuries earlier. It has never been identified on the ground. Egyptian seals and Greek coins from those eras depict the labyrinth in forms that have persisted through subsequent centuries and in widely diverse cultures to the present day.

The nature of the labyrinth is that entry and exit depend on the possession of special knowledge or, what is much the same, special power. The legends that surrounded it originally grew, like all legends, from a basis of facts. The earliest labyrinths were probably intricate buildings or caves put to a defensive use. An enemy feeling his way through their passages and courtyards could be taken by surprise; while an enemy trying to withdraw became confused and lost his way.

The human imagination then made a short leap. From providing protection against actual marauders the labyrinth came to be regarded as a sacred barrier against evil spirits. The tombs of some of the Egyptian kings were constructed with labyrinthine passageways to protect the corpse against harm from the spirit world. At the same time funerary dances in labyrinthine figures were performed to establish a sacred circle round the corpse to preserve its integrity, and like the labyrinth itself the dances persisted in various forms and with changing significance down the centuries into our own Middle Ages and even, as a tradition whose meaning has faded from folk memory, up to the twentieth century on village greens.

The popular legend of the Minotaur in his labyrinth on Crete marked a change of direction for the already age-old myth. Designed by Daedalus, the great artificer, who may or may not have used the method illustrated in Figure 1, the

Figure 1: Construction of classical type of labyrinth from a cross and four dots.

labyrinth was constructed not to protect a god-king but to contain a rapacious monster. Thus in one sense the myth had been turned inside out. Aegeus, King of Athens, had to pay tribute to Minos, King of Crete, in recompense for the murder of Minos's son. The tribute took the form of seven youths and seven maidens being dispatched from Athens every nine years to assuage the appetite of the Minotaur (which had been born of a union between Minos's wife Queen Pasiphae and a bull).

The story of how Theseus, son of Aegeus, penetrated the labyrinth, slew the Minotaur, and found his way back to safety by the thread that Ariadne had given him and which he fastened to the entrance, has enthralled young and old down the centuries as a tale recounting a hero's conquest of the malign power that held his country in thrall – though his conduct on the return journey was unworthy even of a Greek god and caused the death of his father.

So now we have the labyrinth presenting a challenge to the god-hero to save his country from evil rather than protecting the god-king from the evil of the underworld. Thereafter the myth underwent a further transformation, for it was taken over by the early Christians. Labyrinths appeared in the tiled floors of churches as early as the fourth century AD in Algeria and during the first millennium also in a number of Italian churches.[2] Some were depicted on church walls in the early centuries. By medieval times many cathedrals and lesser churches in France had acquired mazes in their paved floors; a famous example survives in Chartres Cathedral, though many have been destroyed. No pavement maze has been identified with certainty in any British church, but in St Mary

Redcliffe, Bristol, there is a fifteenth century carved and painted roof boss in the north aisle showing a maze.

The meander pattern, a common decoration in classical times and subsequently (for example, on the tiles of church floors), can be transformed into a maze by the successive deformations shown in Figure 2.

The appeal of this strikingly pagan symbol to Christians seems odd until one remembers its antecedents. As the repository of the god-king in Egyptian mythology it preserved at its heart a sacred object that could be reached only after a perilous journey, sufficiently perilous to bemuse evil spirits. As the prison of the Minotaur it contained in its fastness an evil power that could be overcome only by heroic adventure. Both these themes have their echoes, incidentally, in the medieval legends of knights beating back the forces of evil as they quested through the forests for that sacred vessel, the Holy Grail.

In the Middle Ages the Christian imagination adapted all this to the idea of a pilgrim's journey to Jerusalem, regarded as being at the centre of the maze, or of a penitential journey

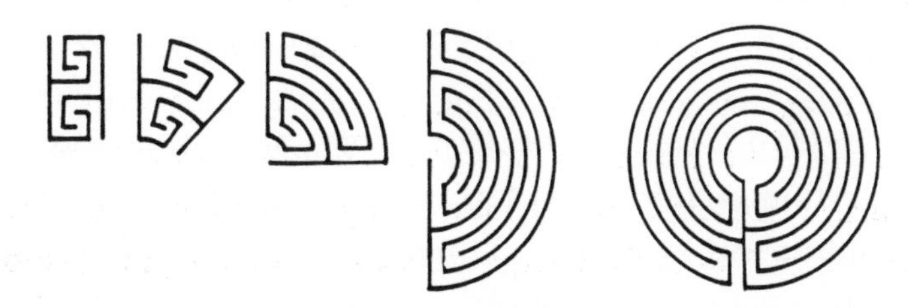

Figure 2: Transformation of the meander pattern into a labyrinth of classical design.

undertaken by a sinner. The practice is supposed to have grown up of sinners slowly and painfully crawling on their knees along the tiled track of a maze in the church pavement, meditating the while on the errors of their ways and given every opportunity to contrast the digressions of their life with the undeviating course they were required to follow along the maze's winding path. Finally they reached its centre, made sacred by the penance they had paid on their journey, and achieved absolution.

At much the same period man's unsleeping imagination now introduced this time-worn symbol to another dramatic role. During the Middle Ages mazes were cut in the turf in England and more rarely in some northern countries of the European continent. Sadly, most have been destroyed by people who saw no point in them; in this country only eight remain, several of them heavily restored, and they cannot be precisely dated. One is in the private grounds of a house and so could be considered an adornment to its garden; it is a particularly fine example, at Troy Farm in Oxfordshire (the association of the city of Troy with mazes is another ramification of the legend). The others are in more or less public areas of grassland. Those that survive vary in diameter (or breadth: one is square) from under 50 feet (15m) to over 100 feet (30m).

Though precise knowledge of how they were used in medieval times is lacking, later traditions suggest that a springtime dance was performed through the maze by local youths to rescue a maiden 'imprisoned' at its centre. Thus by a heroic journey the young men released the fertility of the soil and brought a blessing on the coming summer's crops. The ailing land was restored to health just as the penitent sinner traversing the pavement maze was restored to divine favour, and as Athens was restored to tranquillity when the menace of the Minotaur was lifted.

Another branch of the fertility myth is presumed to have found expression during medieval and later centuries in the construction of several hundred mazes in Scandinavia by means of boulders laid on turf. A similar boulder maze used to overlook the sea on St Agnes, Isles of Scilly, but it was recently replaced by a much criticised 'restoration.'[3] Again, as with the turf mazes, the precise purpose which boulder mazes served is conjectural, but nearly all are near the sea shore, which suggests they may have been the groundwork of a ritual intended to secure the fertility of the sea to fishermen before they set out in their boats.

* * *

Mazes such as the Cretan labyrinth depicted on Greek coins, and the many variations on its design that fulfilled a ritual purpose for the redemption of Christian souls or the release of nature's fertility, were *unicursal.* They had only a single track with no false turnings. So it comes as a surprise to realise that, despite all the mythology surrounding them of a hazardous entry and confusing exit, of a magic force that entangled evil spirits, of a perilous journey to venture on which might be to vanish from the world of men, and of an escape ensured only with the help of Ariadne's thread, it was impossible to lose the way in or out. The power of a unicursal maze is figurative, not structural. It is a sacred symbol, not a defensive redoubt.

Ever since medieval times mazes have been common playthings in the gardens of Europe, especially Italy, France, and England. According to Harvey[4] they were commonplace in English gardens as early as 1494. In Tudor and Jacobean gardens they were elaborate and numerous. These were probably all unicursal. But in the seventeenth century, perhaps owing to Dutch influence,[5] *multicursal* mazes began to appear in gardens. Their paths are branched, and the design may include islands, so that anyone traversing the maze has to choose one way rather than another, with the risk of becoming lost. The oldest surviving hedge maze in Britain is the multicursal one at Hampton Court; it dates from 1690, when it may have replaced an earlier maze on the same site.

Then after fading somewhat from interest in the eighteenth century, garden mazes became popular again in the nineteenth, when many of the large hedge mazes to be seen in gardens today were planted or replanted. Now in the twentieth century enthusiasm for them has again increased, with the result that new ones of ingenious design have recently been constructed in public as well as private gardens.

Nearly all garden mazes depart from the classical design in that they are multicursal. The sacred journey has disappeared. In its place we have a playground where children may run about in hide-and-seek, where grownups may try out their theories of how to thread a maze, and lovers may exchange a kiss when they reach the centre.

★ ★ ★

The best introduction to the history of mazes is the book by Matthews[1] despite its having been published as long ago as 1922. Nigel Pennick[2] has given an excellent modern treatment of the subject. Fisher and Kingham[5] present a short yet thorough conspectus of mazes, well illustrated. For an account of puzzle mazes the reader should turn to Fisher and Gerster,[6] the latter's aerial photographs being specially remarkable. The most scholarly and thought-provoking discussion of the mythology of the labyrinth in Graeco-Roman and Egyptian times is by Jackson Knight.[7] Fisher and Saward[8] have provided a guide to mazes open to the public.

I am indebted to Mr Adrian Fisher (Minotaur Designs) for permission to reproduce Figure 1, and to Mr Nigel Pennick for permission to reproduce Figure 2.

References, Acknowledgements and Index

References

Chapter 1

1 Dean and Chapter, Salisbury. *Salisbury Cathedral and Cathedral Close.* Salisbury. ND

2 This and subsequent quotations from the *Tao Tê Ching* are reproduced from *The Way and its Power*, by Arthur Waley (London: Allen and Unwin. 1934). The authorship of the *Tao Tê Ching* is usually attributed to Lao Tzu, a sage who lived at about 500 BC. It is a compilation of texts from various sources, and Waley dates it to the third century BC.

Chapter 3

1 Walpole H. *The History of the Modern Taste in Gardening.* Ch. 7, On modern gardening. (Facsimile reprint, ed. Hunt J.D.) New York: Garland. 1982.

2 Thomas K. *Man and the Natural World*, p. 265. London: Lane. 1983.

3 Keswick M. *The Chinese Garden*, p. 154. London: Academy Editions. 1978.

Chapter 4

1 Hunt J.D. *William Kent: Landscape Garden Designer*, p. 85. London: Zwemmer. 1987.

2 For illustrations see in particular: Qian Yun, ed. *Classical Chinese Gardens.* Hong Kong and Beijing: Joint Publishing Company, China Building Industry Press. 1982.

Chapter 5

1 Shenstone W. *The Works in Verse and Prose of William Shenstone, Esq.* Unconnected thoughts on gardening, p. 131. (Facsimile reprint, ed. Hunt J.D.) New York: Garland. 1982
2 Peacock T.L. *Headlong Hall*, p. 30. London: Dent (Everyman's Library). 1961.
3 Home of Kames H. *Elements of Criticism*, vol. 1, p. 301. 8th edn. Edinburgh: Bell *et al.* 1807.

Chapter 6

1 Itoh T. *Space and Illusion in the Japanese Garden*, pp. 15–16, 24. New York: Weatherhill/Tankosha. 1973.
2 Ibid., pp. 29–32.
3 Appleton J. *The Experience of Landscape.* Chichester: Wiley and Hull University Press. 1986.
4 Brookes J. *The Small Garden*, p. 16. London: Marshall Cavendish. 1977.
5 Blomfield R. *The Formal Garden in England*, p. 4. London: Macmillan. 1892.

Chapter 7

1 Pottle F.A, ed. *Boswell in Holland 1763–1764*, p. 303. London: Heinemann. 1952.

Chapter 8

1 Sitwell G. *On the Making of Gardens*, pp. 98–99. London: John Murray. 1909.
2 Shenstone W. *The Works in Verse and Prose of William Shenstone, Esq.* Unconnected thoughts on gardening, p. 137. (Facsimile reprint, ed. Hunt J.D.) New York: Garland. 1982.
3 Suzuki D.T. *Zen and Japanese Culture*, p. 370. London: Routledge and Kegan Paul. 1959.

Chapter 9

1 Cecil D. *Library Looking-glass*, p. 47. London: Constable. 1975.
2 Robinson J.M. *Temples of Delight: Stowe Landscape Gardens*. London: Philip and the National Trust. 1990.

Chapter 10

1 Lucas F.L. *The Search for Good Sense*, p. 164. London: Cassell. 1958.
2 Jackson-Stops G. *The Country House Garden: A Grand Tour*, p. 28. London: Pavilion Books and Michael Joseph. 1987.

Chapter 11

1 Loudon J.C. Quoted in: Hadfield M. *A History of British Gardening*, p. 258. London: John Murray. 1960

Chapter 12

1 Anonymous. In: Gardner H. ed. *The New Oxford Book of English Verse, 1250–1950*. Oxford: Oxford University Press. 1972.
2 Strong R. *The Renaissance Garden in England*, p.11. London: Thames and Hudson. 1979.
3 Verulam, Francis Lo. *The Essayes or Counsels, Civill and Morall*. Of gardens. London: Haviland for Barret. 1625.
4 Wotton H. *The Elements of Architecture*. London: Bill. 1624.
5 Clark K. *Landscape into Art*, p. 124. London: John Murray. 1949.
6 Suzuki D.T. *Zen and Japanese Culture*, p. 276. London: Routledge and Kegan Paul. 1959.

Chapter 13

1 Thrale H.L. In: Balderstone KC, ed. *Thraliana: The Diary of Mrs Hester Lynch Thrale (later Mrs Piozzi) 1776–1809*, vol.1, p. 446, fn 4. Oxford: Clarendon Press. 1951.
2 Clark K. *Civilisation*, pp. 290–291. British Broadcasting Corporation and John Murray. 1969.

Chapter 14

1 Shenstone W. *The Works in Verse and Prose of William Shenstone, Esq.* Unconnected thoughts on gardening, p. 130. Facsimile reprint, ed. Hunt J.D.) New York: Garland. 1982.

Appendix 1

1 Ferguson G. *Signs and Symbols in Christian Art.* New York: Oxford University Press. 1966.
2 McLean T. *Medieval English Gardens.* London: Collins. 1981.

Appendix 2

1 Home of Kames H. *Elements of Criticism*, vol. 2, p. 361. 8th edn. London: Vernor and Hood. 1805.

Appendix 4

1 Matthews W.H. *Mazes and Labyrinths: Their History and Development.* (Reprint of 1922 edition published by Longmans, Green.) New York: Dover Publications. 1970.
2 Pennick N. *Mazes and Labyrinths.* London: Robert Hale. 1990.
3 Saward J, Saward D. St Agnes – restoration or destruction? *Caerdroia* 1989; 22: 6–11.
4 Harvey J. *Mediaeval Gardens*, p. 112. London: Batsford. 1981.
5 Fisher A, Kingham D. *Mazes.* Princes Risborough: Shire Publications. 1991.
6 Fisher A, Gerster G. *The Art of the Maze.* London: Weidenfeld and Nicolson. 1990.
7 Knight W.F.J. *Cumaean Gates.* Oxford: Blackwell. 1936.
8 Fisher A, Saward J. *The British Maze Guide.* St Albans: Minotaur Designs. 1991.

Acknowledgments

For permission to quote passages from the books shown in parentheses I am indebted to the following publishers: Academy Group (*The Chinese Garden*, by Maggie Keswick); BBC Enterprises Ltd (*Civilisation*, by Kenneth Clark); Constable (*Library Looking-Glass*, by David Cecil); Unwin Hyman of HarperCollins (*The Way and its Power*, by Arthur Waley); Marshall Cavendish (*The Small Garden*, by John Brookes); Octopus Publishing Group Library and Martin Secker & Warburg (*The Magic Mountain*, by Thomas Mann); Penguin Books (*Man and the Natural World*, by Keith Thomas); Thames and Hudson (*The Renaissance Garden in England*, by Roy Strong); Yale University (*Boswell in Holland 1763–1764*, edited by F. A. Pottle). For bibliographical assistance I am grateful to Mrs Hazel Fallon, and to St Andrews University Library (Mrs C. M. Gascoigne) and Exeter University Library (Mr J. Stirling). For helpful comments on the typescript I am grateful to my wife and our daughter Katherine.

Index